TRUMPED

IN

AMERICA

Reflections on How Fascism Grows

J. Wayne Frye

This book is written in Canadian English

Trumped in America:
Reflections on How Fascism Grows

TO: Those poor souls who fall for the propaganda spewed out by their masters who effectively manipulate them by waving the American flag and shouting Jesus. The poor souls simply line up willingly for their balls and chains. Some people actually enjoy being slaves.

Cover Illustration by Michael Vadon PhotoStream (2016)

COPYRIGHT 2018
BY
J. WAYNE FRYE

Catalogue Number: 971688-2018

ISBN: 978-1-928183-37-2

An Educational Research Associates Primer
Distributed By
Fireside Books – Canadian Division
Part of the Peninsula Publishing Consortium

Trumped in America:
Reflections on How Fascism Grows

TABLE OF CONTENTS

Trumped in America:
Reflections on How Fascism Grows

About the Author

This is a rare non-fiction book from Dr. Wayne Frye who wrote the award winning *How Hockey Saved a Jew from the Holocaust: The Rudi Ball Story*. His *Aaron Adams* mysteries, *Chablis Louise Chavez* thrillers, *Girl* books and *Lynton* adventures titillate the brains of those who enjoy tantalizing tales. His life has been filled with adventure and excitement. He has been a college hockey coach, professor, and at one time, the youngest university president in the USA. Called a marketing genius by the *Los Angeles Times*, he has been a promotional consultant to hockey teams and motion picture companies. He has been cited for his work with inner-city gangs in Los Angeles and is active in the anti-globalization movement. A proud Canadian, he divides his time between Ladysmith, British Columbia and Cape Town, South Africa. He provides satirical political commentary to many Canadian newspapers.

Some of the 46 books by J. Wayne Frye

Hockey Mania and the Mystery of Nancy Running Elk
Something Evil in the Darkness at Hopkins House
White Meteors and the Ghost of Sue Ann McGee
How Hockey Saved a Jew From the Holocaust
The Girl Who Said Goodbye for the Last Time
The Girl Who Motivated Murder Most Foul
The Girl Who Stirred up the Whirlwind
The Girl Who Rode into a Storm
Sammy Sasquatch and the Sts'ailes Star
Fall From Apocalypse
Armageddon Now
Worth Part 1: Roaring Through Life Like a Comet in the Midnight Sky
Worth Part 2: The Night of Thunder Road
When Jesus Came to Jersey as the Son of Thunder
When Jesus Came to Canada to Lead an Indigenous Rebellion
When Jesus Came to the Black Hills to do the Ghost Dance
Lynton Walks on Water
Lynton Curls Her Hair
Lynton and the Vampire at Tagaytay Manor
Lynton Buys a Cell-Phone and Hears the Voice of Doom
Lynton Viñas and Beowulf Perez in the Taal Inferno
Lynton and the Ghosts in the Mansion on Balete Drive
Lynton Viñas: Shadow in the Darkness
Lynton's South African Adventure
Lynton, the Karoo Vampire and the Jewels of Omar Bin Abi
Lynton and the Stellenbosch Terror
Chablis: Avenging Angel for the Forgotten
In the City of Lost Hope
Chablis and the Terrorist
Pursuit
The Disappearance

Trumped in America:
Reflections on How Fascism Grows

Prologue

Put Your Hand on Your Billfold

In 2003 I finally gave up on the USA, crossed the border into Canada and never looked back. I did it because I could no longer tolerate the drift toward fascism that had occurred under both Democrats and Republicans. I knew instinctively that the appointment by the biased Supreme Court of George W. Bush as President was putting a man in charge with no inner moral compass. The September 11, 2001 terrorist attack inexorably led

Trumped in America:
Reflections on How Fascism Grows

the sheep-like Americans down the road of fascism as they embraced torture as acceptable when waging war against Muslims.

I can remember my father once saying back when I was a child in 1960 that Dwight Eisenhower proved to the world that the USA didn't need a President, because it had functioned for eight years without one. Ironically, it took the assassination of John F. Kennedy in 1963 that made Lyndon Johnson President to actually get effective social legislation through Congress, as Johnson was a far more effective legislator than Kennedy. Unfortunately, ever since then, the Republicans have fought vehemently to dismantle all Johnson's programmes and continued their attempt to dismantle FDR's New Deal that they started fighting in 1933. The Republicans simply have no compassion or concern for anyone but the rich. Still, it is often the poor and the elderly who vote for them as they are seen as the party that loves Jesus the most.

J. Wayne Frye

Trumped in America:
Reflections on How Fascism Grows

This is not just a book about the extreme fascism of Donald Trump, as much as it is a book about the fond embracing of subliminal fascism by gullible, uncompassionate Americans who think there is more harm done by a football player kneeling for the National Anthem than by an out-of-control President urging the snatching of immigrant babies from their mothers' arms so they can be locked up in separate cages provided by corporations reaping rewards off human misery. Corporations were also complicit in the killing of Jews in Nazi Germany, as capitalism knows no bounds when it comes to the bottom line. These monoliths of evil are the prime movers behind instilling patriotic fervour by spewing propaganda to the public about how grand America is compared to the rest of the world. This is the very reason impressionable American youths, who are forced to stand and recite the Pledge of Allegiance every morning in school and dutifully sing the National Anthem, after thorough patriotic

Trumped in America:
Reflections on How Fascism Grows

brainwashing by history teachers, line up to fight wars of conquest while the children and grandchildren of the wealthy laugh all the way to cash another check from their trust funds.

The material in this small volume barely scratches the surface of a problem which is increasingly perilous for Americans as the activities of disguised fascists in the United States are on the rise, and in fact, since the election of Donald Trump, many fascists are brazen enough now to admit their proclivities toward white supremacy and the institution of rule by the oligarchy which has seized control of a nation that is not only the most warlike, but by far the most hypocritical on the face of the earth.

During the short time Trump has been at the head of the U.S. government, the crudely organized and directed propaganda machine developed in concert with the most corrupt, narcissistic, self-nerving President in history, aided by *Fox News*, has grown in influence far

Trumped in America:
Reflections on How Fascism Grows

wider than most people seem to realize. What at first appeared to be merely a distasteful attempt by Trump officials and their Russian allies at direct interference in the affairs of the American people and their government has now assumed the more sinister aspect of emboldening those who harbour deep-rooted prejudice against any non-whites and non-English speakers. Meanwhile, the militarized police have been given free reign to ruthlessly slay people of colour with impunity, while the Gestapo-similar ICE agents, prancing around like the SS in Nazi Germany, are grabbing babies from mother's arms. These are the very people, along with the patriotically blind Trump-loving supporters, who would gladly march illegal immigrants off to internment camps and cheerfully dance to the tunes of Wagner while they were being gassed. They, in most cases, will also tell you how much they love Jesus and how they long for America to somehow find its path to God again. Ironically, some of the most ardent proponents for Trump and Jesus are the corporations, which we all know have America's best interests at heart. Evangelicals are among some of Trump's most vehement supporters, as it should be obvious that the misogynistic, bigoted, narcissistic President is among God's chosen, according to these flag-waving, hypocritical Christians who never saw a fascist Jesus worshipper they did not love.

The embrace of Trump is nearly universal among evangelical leaders who pander to humanities' basest instincts. Religion, in the USA, is not on the side of the poor, the downtrodden or the miserable. Religion is nothing more than a giant corporation that rakes in billions from the gullible while paying no taxes. I fondly recall my dear grandfather telling me when I was a child: "Son, if a man tells you he is a Christian, put your hand on your billfold."

Trumped in America:
Reflections on How Fascism Grows

Chapter 1

A Pit of Despair

In a few European countries, especially in Czechoslovakia, just before that republic was turned over to Germany's mercy by the Munich Peace Accord of 1938, and in France where Nazi and Italian agents built an amazing secret underground army, there was the same type of clandestine involvement there as in the 2016 election by Russian cyber-spies to make sure a compliant government was put in power in the

Trumped in America:
Reflections on How Fascism Grows

USA. In 2016, the Russian government used modern technology to infiltrate what was left of the fragile American democracy and tilt the election in Donald Trump's favour. In fact, it was even more blatant than Germany's meddling in countries' elections prior to 1940.

Vladimir Putin is a master manipulator, who has played Trump like a fine tuned Stradivarius, utilizing Trump's need for aggrandizement to massage his fragile ego as a result of deep rooted feelings of inferiority due to his father's looking upon him as a moron who always needed to be bailed out of failing enterprises. This is the same father who may have been a contributor to his other son Fred's addictive personality that led to death at only 43 from drug and alcohol abuse. I am not a psychologist, so I will not explore what is seemingly a family trait of personality disorder that afflicted Fred Trump and possibly Donald Trump, but suffice it to say that Donald is a man who shows signs of harbouring deep personal

Trumped in America:
Reflections on How Fascism Grows

demons that play upon a fragile mind. In the process, he has such a shallow character that he bullies all who dare stand against his narcissistic impulses. This is a man, who, as long as he knows he and the immediate members of his family will be safe, would have no remorse in ordering a catastrophic nuclear attack on any country.

I have lived through 13 presidencies, and along with Richard Nixon, Trump has perfected the use of the government as a criminal enterprise more effectively than anyone I can remember. Many of Nixon's henchmen wound up in jail, but that was a time when the nation was not so ideological divided, and it was also a time when Congress was able to ameliorate differences long enough to pursue a modicum of justice.

The creeping fascism of America is almost complete now that Trump wound up as President, despite losing the popular vote by over three million. This has happened five times in American history, and the USA still has the gall to call itself a democracy. This antiquated method of choosing a leader diminishes the value of each person's vote. Add that to the practice of gerrymandering (drawing congressional district maps to benefit one party), and you have the complete prescription for disenfranchisement, which has been used by both parties to ensure the perpetuation of their power.

The USA is considered a pariah by most nations of the world. Long ago (with Vietnam), America lost its moral compass, and is now seen by most people in other countries to be a cesspool of hypocrisy, as it talks peace and love while using its military machine to roll across the world to serve corporate interests. With a military budget that exceeds the next 11 countries combined, it neglects education, healthcare and poverty to feed this monster that is devouring the nation with a voracious appetite that cannot be satiated.

Finally, with the election of Donald Trump, the USA has no claim to moral superiority, as the 35

Trumped in America:
Reflections on How Fascism Grows

to 42 percent of brainwashed Trump-adoring worshippers of hypocrisy have embraced fascism with glee as they have no problem locking children in cages or denying health care to millions who are dying for lack of compassion, while the government hands billionaires tax cuts.

Among the First World nations, and many Third World countries, only the USA has heartless, uncaring for-profit healthcare, where the corporate bottom-line comes before people, and this is in a country that dares to call itself a Christian nation. What would these Christians beloved Jesus think of a nation that allows people to die on hospital steps because they do not have insurance? This kind of abomination reflects the uncaring nature of these people who praise Jesus while turning their backs on everything he stood for. Of course, hypocrisy is the norm for so many evangelicals that one can almost understand why they would embrace Trump as he wallows in hypocrisy and bathes his followers with his sanctimonious

Trumped in America:
Reflections on How Fascism Grows

rhetoric assailing non-whites as vermin that are infesting America. It is understandable that Trump might relish Hitler's *My New Order*, as he has used the speeches in that book just as effectively as did Hitler. Trump's loyal, worshipful followers would have been right at home in 1930's Germany vilifying the Jews. They would probably have gotten a real high out of watching Jews, Gypsies, the mentally challenged, the handicapped and homosexuals being herded into cattle cars.

One cannot fully understand today's romance with fascism by so many Americans without first understanding just how fascism gets a hold on a nation through the gradual amalgamation of power by an oligarchy that sees people as commodities that can be used, abused and then discarded after they have served the needs of corporations.

Fascism was founded in Italy by Benito Mussolini, who began his political career as a socialist but eventually embraced the idea of an authoritarian, nationalist, corporate state to

Trumped in America:
Reflections on How Fascism Grows

achieve his goals, as he saw the oligarchy as a means to achieve his ultimate aim of unchallenged personal power. Unlike Lenin, Mussolini's ideology did not include international revolution, stressing instead the unity and glory of the Italian nation and the dangers posed to the country and its culture by Communist-inspired workers' revolts. He felt giving workers power would diminish the ability of the state to accomplish its fascist aims. Like the modern day Trump phenomena, his brand of fascism was developed through a radical political movement supported by just enough of the population to assure his hold on power by emphasizing discipline and devotion to nativism along with faith in an authoritarian figure supported by the oligarchy. This made fascism far more palatable to traditional elements of society, such as business interests and the church that saw in it a means to organize the working and middle classes to defend their interests against outsiders. Mussolini chose the title *Duce* (leader) and modelled his image on the emperors of ancient Rome, developing a cult of personality around himself. Italians, reeling from what they saw as too much foreign influence and fear of communism, bowed humbly before this charlatan and con man who knew how to manipulate the gullible.

Mussolini's beliefs influenced many others during the mid-Twentieth Century, namely Adolf Hitler, Britain's Oswald Moseley and Spain's General Francisco Franco. Even Britain's Winston Churchill was an early admirer of Mussolini's rule in Italy.

Mussolini erroneously believed that he could make the Italian economy completely self-sufficient in spite of its lack of natural resources. Eventually, this led to an expansionist foreign policy and the search for those resources through war in North Africa. Even in the 1930's, the world was already becoming interdependent and it has continued down that path ever since, and despite

Trumped in America:
Reflections on How Fascism Grows

Trump's posturing and the imposition of tariffs to keep out foreign goods, all this will lead to is lower wages for Americans and higher prices because the USA is no longer the dominant power in the world. Italy found out the hard way that trade barriers on resources only lead to stagnant wages and higher prices.

In the USA, the recent Supreme Court decisions against unionization and the approval for corporations to buy elections guarantees that Americans are going to receive lower and lower wages when adjusted for inflation, fewer benefits and longer hours while faced with rising prices as the cycle of greed in capitalism never allows for the realization that putting more money into the hands of workers is beneficial to corporations. Put money in a working man's pocket and the rich will have it by the end of the day.

With the Trumping of America, the national debt will explode as a result of tax cuts, a consolidation of corporations will make them even more powerful and in the end all this will lead to a greater crash than the one caused by a moron almost as ignorant as Trump. George W. Bush's malfeasance almost completely destroyed the American economy.

A careful look at despots who are admired by Trump may offer a gaze into the crystal ball of tomorrow when the bill for the folly of voting for Donald Trump will be delivered to the American people. Unfortunately, those who did not vote for him will also suffer the consequences, but you can be assured, just as they were with Obama, the corporations and barons of greed on Wall Street will be bailed out by the U.S. government. Gullible Americans shout the praises of capitalism, but they are too manipulated to see that for the rich and corporations, socialism is the norm, because while the government will let the working men and women starve on the streets, it will always come to the rescue of those at the top of the economic ladder.

Trumped in America:
Reflections on How Fascism Grows

Through it all, Trump and his family will be the ones that receive the greatest largesse from a system every bit as sinister as that utilized by Hitler. Looking at Hitler's aims indicates a man of superior intellect to Trump, but their intentions are similar, and in the end, the intellectually challenged Trump, through his worshipping hordes and their acquiescence to his skilful manipulation, will bring about calamity.

Hitler succeeded because he was able to rearm Germany and once World War II began he was able to keep the country functioning. Hitler's political movement, National Socialism, was like today's Republican Party, uniquely acquiescent in its anti-Semitic, anti-immigrant focus and its devotion to the ideal of the Aryans (Northern Europeans) as a superior race, an idea often not absent from other forms of fascism. Today, although Jews are still vilified by Trump's Republican enablers; the Blacks, Hispanics and immigrants are at the top of the list for vilification as vermin infesting a white, Christian nation. The Jews, this time, are a bit lower down on the ladder of bigoted blame, but they are still disparaged nonetheless by Trump supporters.

Hitler and Mussolini both looked at the concentration camps utilized by the British, with the support of Churchill, in the Boar War in South Africa, and the dismal Indian Reservations used in the USA as prototypes for the incarceration and elimination of undesirables as the Nazis took the fiendishness to unimaginable heights. Fascism also engaged in imperialism and the expansion of territory; Mussolini invaded Ethiopia while Hitler invaded the rest of Europe and North Africa, just like the USA invades country after country as a result of its sick adherence to an idea of moral superiority. Even Obama carried out crimes against humanity with his drone strikes that killed thousands of innocents. The USA simply has no boundaries in its deplorable assault on humanity all across the globe.

Trumped in America:
Reflections on How Fascism Grows

Today, as Trump embraces dictatorships and disparages old democratic alliances, one can reflect on the shifting alliances of pre-World War II. The influence of Nazi ideology upon England's now notorious *Cliveden Set*, which manoeuvred the betrayal of Austria, sacrificed Czechoslovakia and worked to strengthen Hitler throughout Europe, had so profound an effect upon the growth and influence of fascism throughout the world that it offered a precursor to the calamity that followed. Today, Trump, with the world's mightiest nuclear arsenal at his disposal loves to play the intimidation game just as Hitler did.

Much of the material in this volume has been published before in various periodicals, but so many Americans now embrace creeping Fascism that little of what is detailed here will have an effect on people who will not read this book, but rather, will rely on the Trump mouthpiece, Fox News, for all their information. About 35% to 42% of Americans today have their heads buried in the sands of hypocrisy and simply will not seek out any other source but conservative talk radio and Fox TV News for their political information. This makes reasonable discourse with these people impossible.

There was a time when all broadcast stations had to be fair and balanced, even offer opposing views through the equal time provisions of the Communications Act. Ronald Reagan, who started the decline of civility and fairness in media by eliminating the Fairness Doctrine, saw to it that an era when broadcasters had to be fair and balanced was tossed into the dust bin of history so news outlets and talk radio could toe the conservative line and eschew any semblance of rationally fair analysis.

I left the USA in 2003 because I could see where things were headed with George Bush's lies and deceit which were, at that time, being used to beat the drums of war against Iraq. Any reasonably intelligent person could see the spectre of fascism

Trumped in America:
Reflections on How Fascism Grows

in the vilification of Muslims and the embrace of
the trickle down theory of economics from the
Reagan era which Republicans have clung to like
a drowning man to a life jacket. The belief that
somehow, if you give the rich more money they
will miraculously let it trickle down to the poor is
about as likely as the earth being proved to be flat.
That is why fascist penetration in the USA grows
each and every day because of the ignorance of so
many who actually believe that a wealthy,
narcissistic, egotistical, conceited, self-serving
buffoon like Trump will somehow represent the
interests of the working men and women. I do not
know which is worse – Trump or his worshipping
throng of adherents that blindly follow him over
his precipice of vanity that will trap them in a pit
of economic ruin and moral turpitude.

Trumped in America:
Reflections on How Fascism Grows

Even the physical mannerisms of Trump compare

to those of other despots.

Trumped in America:
Reflections on How Fascism Grows

Chapter 2

Forever Extinguished the Light of Hope

When the Spanish insurgents were steaming into Madrid early in November, 1936, insurgent General Emilio Mola referred to the fascist sympathizers within Madrid, those attempting to thoroughly defeat the Spanish Government by means of spying, sabotage and terrorism, as the Fifth Column, which is the term widely used ever since then to describe the various fascist and Nazi organizations operating within the borders of a nation. Today, the Republican Party is in the hands of corporations and the wealthy (Fifth Column) and enthusiastically does their bidding. Unfortunately, they are aided and abetted by a Democratic Party that is little better.

In order to better understand how fascism has steadily grown in the USA, we must first parallel it to what happened with Germany before the beginning of World War II, because the USA is the modern Nazi Germany today, using threats and when that does not work, utilizing its vast military might to subdue those that stand in the way of its determination to secure the entire world for exploitation by capitalist terrorists. The term democracy in America is nothing but a code word for exploitation by the moneyed class. People are simply too brainwashed to realize that when you are denied a living wage, food, shelter, education and health care that there is no democracy for the masses. Unfortunately, the easily brainwashed in the United States of America have been

Trumped in America:
Reflections on How Fascism Grows

conditioned to respond like Pavlov's dog every time the bell of patriotism is rung. Wave the flag, shout Jesus and people snap to attention, believing they are living in the greatest nation on earth. The truth is that they are living in one of the most brainwashed nations on earth, where the masses are so easily manipulated that they actually steadfastly believe the propaganda spewed out by the corporate controlled news media and the government.

Any truly critical thinker should see Trump's aim is similar to Hitler's, as he attacks old alliances and blames other nations for the lack of opportunity in the USA, a lack of opportunity actually caused by an American government that feeds the voracious appetites of those at the top of the economic ladder while callously ignoring those in the middle and at the bottom.

The 35 to 42 percent of the American people who idolize Trump are no different than those who worshipped Hitler and Mussolini. They are simply

Trumped in America:
Reflections on How Fascism Grows

caught up on the cult of personality and cannot see that they are feeding the monster that will eventually devour them. The irony is that most of the people who adore Trump are actually deplored by him. He sees them as ignorant cretins that are easily manipulated. He has, on several occasions long before running for President, intonated that Republican voters are the easiest to manipulate and fool. Likewise, Hitler and Mussolini knew exactly what people they could easily fool.

Trump, sensing his base as celebrity worshipping, easily manipulated non-thinkers who respond to racist, flag-waving, patriotic, absurd, nonsensical rhetoric was able to effectively motivate them through emotional appeals to blindly fall in line in support of his "drain the swamp" appeals. He blatantly said, "I like uneducated people," because he assumed people capable of critical thinking would see through his shallowness, unintelligible speech, race-baiting and outright buffoonery. His mastery of the

J. Wayne Frye

electoral map along with the support of the people whom he would throw under the bus economically, was a winning formula in a nation that does not elect the person who wins the most votes, but rather the one who gets the most strategic (electoral) votes state by state. That is why a man who lost the election by three million votes is now immersing the nation in fascism.

Ironically, while Trump passed tax cuts that benefitted the wealthy, his poor and middle class base that reap no real rewards from the tax cut still cheer him on enthusiastically. These people are so easily brainwashed that they are unable to realize they are voting against their own self-interests. It is amazing that people who struggle to put food on their tables are more concerned about stopping abortion, keeping their guns and praying in school than eating. This is the kind of mentality played upon by Republicans who wrap themselves in the flag, Jesus and the Constitution while trampling on all three to serve the interests of the rich and powerful. Just as Trump said, his supporters would still worship at his altar even if he shot someone at high noon on Fifth Avenue. These are the same kind of people who supported Hitler and Mussolini with undying devotion. There are a large percentage of people who simply want someone to do their thinking for them, and these are the people who have cast their lot with Trump. His narcissism, his "pussy grabbing," his utter disdain for the rule of law, his worship of money is of no concern to those who look upon him as their saviour. How unfortunate that when these people have no Medicare in old age, no social security and no social safety net whatsoever they will still be manipulated to the point of blaming Democrats for their plight rather than rich-loving Republicans. Of course, they will be able to worship Jesus freely, so maybe praying to him after Trump is long gone may help. I doubt it!

How then do demagogues like Mussolini, Hitler and Trump sway so many people to support them?

Trumped in America:
Reflections on How Fascism Grows

Figures are hard to come by, as polling was not really done in the 1930's and 1940's in Germany, but estimates of Hitler's support by the Germans, according to many studies, was never above 35% to 40%. The figures were actually a little less for Mussolini.

So, these two, like Trump, never had majority support. However, you do not need majority support if you control all aspects of government, which Hitler and Mussolini did, and which Trump is slowly accomplishing with the precision of a skilled surgeon with scalpel in hand. He is remaking the Supreme Court as a result of the hypocrisy of Senator Mitch McConnell, and when the impeachment question comes up, the Supreme Court will be in his back pocket. Ditto for Congress, the FBI, the CIA, etc. Americans have sat idly by while their government has been turned over to a pack of billionaire fascists who are no longer hiding in the shadows while pulling the strings of their puppet government, but have brought their intentions to make America into a fascist oligarchy out into the sunshine, where they are bathing themselves in the warmth of what they love most – power and money. Meanwhile, the 35% to 42% of Trump lovers have their heads buried in the sand.

Unfortunately, it is not just the USA that is going to suffer, but the whole world. America has always been the world's bully, but now, with Trump at the helm, the school yard bully has his hand on the nuclear button.

In order to understand what is happening today, as alluded to earlier, we must go back in time and see exactly how a man far more cunning than Trump was able to bring the world to the brink of annihilation. Trump is not nearly as intelligent as Hitler was, but he knows how to appeal to the basest instincts of a group that would literally follow him of a cliff into a ravine of misery. His base of support is primarily made up of disaffected middle, lower-middle and poor class whites. These are the people who have seen, since the days of Ronald Reagan actually praising greed as an enviable trait, the complete deterioration of their lifestyles. Wages have stagnated for almost 40 years now under Democrats and Republicans. Working men and women have simply been sacrificed for the good of the 1% who reap vast rewards on the backs of working men and women who toil in obscurity for less and less. Still, these people have been brainwashed into believing someone like Donald Trump (an assumed billionaire) is actually going to help them. It was also the common working-class Germans who believed that Hitler would lift them from the depths of despair caused by a draconian peace treaty forced on them by the victorious allies after World War I. They were every bit as delusional as the Trump supporters are.

So, let's analyze just how Hitler was able to rise to power and lead the people down the path to misery through extreme nationalism that was very

Trumped in America:
Reflections on How Fascism Grows

similar to what Trump is now offering the American people. It is generally admitted that the Munich Peace Agreement gave Germany industrial and military areas essential to further aggressions. Instead of helping to put a troubled Europe on the road to lasting peace, Munich strengthened the totalitarian powers, especially in Germany, and a strengthened Germany inevitably meant increased activities of the Nazis Fifth Column which was, in all quarters of the globe, actively preparing the ground for Hitler's greater plans. Does not the current President (Trump) of the USA employ the same deceptive hand in preparing the world for the rise of American fascism? Excuse me, maybe the correct phrasing would be "the expansion of American fascism," because it has had a strong toe-hold in America for nearly forty years now, and has been gradually and methodically expanding as a result of media concentration in the hands of six corporations, and Fox News, in particular, along with Sinclair

Trumped in America:
Reflections on How Fascism Grows

Broadcasting. In almost every aspect of American life, the spread of conservative propaganda has had little restraint in brainwashing the American public to accept a totalitarian leader, save the more enlightened urban enclaves that have managed to embrace progressiveness and stave off a bit of the unrelenting march of fascist thought.

If we can divine the future by the past, the Fifth Column today is that shadowy group of secret United States capitalist provocateurs now overtly and clandestinely entrenched in every important country throughout the world. It is an omen of what is to come from the world's biggest bully nation, the USA, and the individual bully (Trump) who is now in control of it.

Before Germany marched into Austria, that unhappy country witnessed a large influx of Fifth Column members, just as today the USA has its agents of suppression fanning out all across the globe, but, more importantly, infiltrating every nook and cranny of America itself, where anyone who dares speak against Trump is singled out as unpatriotic. Trump's bluster, bullying and uncompromising attitude, backed by his allies, is simply laying the groundwork for an American order, with no pretence of fairness, that will crush the hopes of working men and women everywhere to get even a modicum of economic justice.

I spent the majority of my young life having to listen to a steady diet of American propaganda. Coming up in the rural south, where I was forced to blindly stand every morning with hand over heart to mindlessly recite the Pledge of Allegiance, each time I ended with the phrase "with liberty and justice for all," I looked around the segregated classroom, and wondered if African-Americans felt there was justice for all. My young mind was pulled in two directions. One direction was the grand southern traditions that I was taught by relatives, friends and teachers who glorified a society that kept millions enslaved to their white masters. This pained my young mind.

Trumped in America:
Reflections on How Fascism Grows

As a descendent of General Robert E. Lee (my mother was a Lee), I was taught to be proud of my heritage. However, I was also pulled in another direction by a grandmother who saw through the self-serving bigotry promulgated by an insular society that could not face up to the reality of a treasonous past where the most heinous of institutions (slavery) was so thoroughly ingrained that thirteen states succeeded from the union to defend the abomination that kept African-Americans in chains to serve the economic interests of their white masters.

To this very day, many in the Southern USA are inexorably still fighting that war, and Donald Trump has manipulated and played on their prejudices against non-whites to form a solid base in the southern states among those who still believe in the supremacy of the white race. As the USA moves toward a white minority in the coming years, the last agonizing pains of the racists that permeate this region are crying out to be saved from the black and brown hordes they feel will destroy their privileged status. This region, along with most Midwestern states, forms a solid nucleus in support of a fascist government that aggrandizes Trump as the "dear leader" who will save the white race. This is the very same type manoeuvre utilized by Mussolini and Hitler to capture the hearts and minds of just enough people to consolidate their power for the nefarious purposes which buttressed their fascist aims.

Each day in the USA, the agents of fascism consolidate their power, and with two appointments to the Supreme Court, giving it a 5-4 conservative majority, Trump has insulated himself and the oligarchy against any assault on their power. At the same time, through intimidation and appointments, Trump is steadily politicizing the FBI, CIA and Department of Justice to assure there is no bulwark of justice to stand against the fascism that is thoroughly embraced by the aforementioned 35% to 42% of

Trumped in America:
Reflections on How Fascism Grows

the American population who obsequiously worship at Trump's altar of hypocrisy and lies.

Each day, Trump's secret army of rich, privileged oligarchs engage in new methods to enslave all to the greed of the 1%. Their numbers are vast and they are methodically taking control of all levels of government with an acquiescing Republican Party that sees the poor as the enemy and the rich as the exalted in a society where poverty increases more rapidly than any other country in the world. The Republican Party may be the fascist's dream, but it is aided and abetted by a Democratic Party that has also been compromised by selling its soul to the corporations and the rich who provide the money needed to get elected in a nation where the number of votes received has a direct correlation to the amount of money collected.

None of this is coincidental. It is a carefully planned strategy from the oligarchy to assure their complete mastery of the political process to protect their interests at the expense of the working men and women, many of whom are lining up like sheep being led to the slaughter pen, brainwashed into believing in an America that does not exist.

In the end, everything boils down to resources to fuel the machinery of greed. For years Hitler had laid plans to fight if he had to for Czechoslovakia, whose natural mountain barriers and man-made defensive line of steel and concrete stood in the way of his announced drive to the Ukrainian wheat fields (resources). In preparation for the day when he might have to fight for its control, he sent into that country a host of spies, provocateurs, propagandists and saboteurs to establish themselves, make contacts, carry on propaganda and build a cadre of evil which would be invaluable in time of war. The USA is doing this today, not only all over the world, but right within its own territory, as any opposition to Trump is seen as a direct attack on the oligarchy.

J. Wayne Frye

Trumped in America:
Reflections on How Fascism Grows

The fascists inexorable determination and their inhuman indifference to the lives of even their own agents shows the depth of depravity in a nation that simply cannot see how the rest of the world is moving forward while it moves backward in order to protect the rich and privileged.

One of the most despicable organizations on American soil is ICE. Like the Gestapo, it is ripping children from mothers' arms and locking them up in corporate run cages in what amounts to concentration camps. Trump has been restrained enough not to despatch the mothers, fathers and children to the ovens yet, but his diehard supporters would, no doubt, enthusiastically endorse this solution to the immigration problem if Trump were emboldened enough to embrace "the final solution."

The far-flung Gestapo (ICE) network in America concentrates much of its activities along the Mexican-USA border. After all, why worry about the Canadian border as what Canadian would want to illegally cross the border and give up their higher wages, almost free university educations, free healthcare, better retirement benefits, one year paid maternity leaves, higher standard of living and a host of other social amenities that Americans can only dream about?

Trump agents make inaccurate reports on public opinion and attitudes to puff up Trump's need for aggrandizement, as massaging his over-sized ego is at the psychological centre of these individuals who will sacrifice their integrity for a seat at the table of privilege. Watching Trump's Director of Communications, Sarah Sanders, blatantly provide her own lies in defence of Trump's lies provides a double whammy of disingenuousness as the real fake news comes not from the media, but from the White House and its propaganda organ, Fox News.

The United States is now led by a man bereft of Christian virtues but still vehemently supported by evangelicals who exhibit hypocrisy of its highest

Trumped in America:
Reflections on How Fascism Grows

form by embracing this cretin of demonic despair.
Trump's Twitter account is a testament to his
dearth of self-mastery or prudence as he extols the
strength of dictators and laments that he has his
own power checked by two other branches of
government. His political ideals are like a
cancerous growth in the heart of the body of
democracy, and this insidious cancer is rapidly
spreading as those who could treat it acquiesce to
the machinations of a mad man. The Republican
Party is willingly watching as this disease
insidiously devours the body politic and destroys
hope.

Trump's warped values impose conformity,
order and authoritarian strength more than
freedom or liberty. He values men more than
women, whites more than Hispanics and African-
Americans, his evangelical enablers more than
real Chrsirians and his personal needs more than
the nation's needs. His ugly, bombastic rhetoric
stirs the basest of human instincts, encouraging

violence, judgementalism, hypocrisy and prejudice.

Trump's entire public life has been predicated on the unapologetic pursuit of self-interest, lust, adultery, greed, lies, bankruptcies and sordid behaviour that is supported by so-called Christians who speak in opposition to those things but embrace it when practiced by Trump. The mockery he makes of everything that indicated a value based society has led to the dismantling of friendships with allies and democratic peoples to the point that whatever moral character is left of a nation that has been creeping toward fascism since the presidency of Ronald Reagan is now on the precipice of a dark pit that will devour a country that for far too long has preached about its freedom while hypocritically investing in the suppression of freedom throughout the world in order to promulgate its culture of greed. Trump is simply the ultimate buffoonish poster child for the hypocrisy practiced by a bullying nation that long

Trumped in America:
Reflections on How Fascism Grows

ago lost its moral compass in pursuit of world domination for its sick and evil economic system.

In this nation where an oligarchy has managed to clandestinely seize power through the acquiescence of the Supreme Court that ruled in the Citizens United Case that corporations and the wealthy were allowed to buy politicians, the dark veil of deceit has possibly forever extinguished the light of hope.

CAPITALISTS MAKE MONEY
THE OLD FASHIONED WAY

THEY INHERIT IT LIKE TRUMP DID

AMERICAN CAPITALISM
TRUMP STYLE

Chapter 3

Fascism Has Arrived in America

The 1933 Reichstag fire shows how quickly a modern republic can be transformed into an authoritarian regime. (The fire was used as evidence by the Nazi Party that communists were plotting against the German government.) The event is seen as pivotal in the establishment of Nazi Germany. This is nothing new, to be sure, in the politics of exception and exclusion. The American Founding Fathers knew that the democracy they were creating was vulnerable to an aspiring tyrant who might seize upon some dramatic event as grounds for the suspension of Constitutional rights, and they thought they had built in safeguards, but they never visualized the propaganda machines like Fox News, Sinclair Broadcasting and right-wing talk radio that would be used to brainwash Americans into blindly supporting fanatical, dogmatic bigotry and intense nationalism.

9/11 was used by George Bush and his henchmen to manipulate Americans into agreeing to actually give up some of their freedoms to defend freedom. These are the same people who decried terrorism, but then used terrorism to fight terrorism. The draconian Patriotic Act, which was passed after the attack on the World Trade Centre, was used to justify torture of Muslims as young as 15. Drone attacks were ratified as justifiable and used by Bush and then Obama to kill countless innocent civilians. The Department of Homeland

Trumped in America:
Reflections on How Fascism Grows

Security, which was instituted by Bush, fostered the American Gestapo (ICE - Immigrations and Customs Enforcement), which, like its German predecessor, the S.S., is rounding up non-white undocumented aliens for deportation and jailing without trial. This organization has been bolstered by Trump who wants to *Make America White Again.*

In 1879, Mark Twain satirically suggested himself for the Presidency, much in the same way that Trump did. He thought it grand hyperbole, but over 150 years later, we have Trump who admitted to "grabbing 'um by the pussy," and was still embraced by his fanatical base that never saw a hypocrite that they did not love. To paraphrase Twain in regards to Trump: *I have pretty much made up my mind to run for President. What the country wants is a candidate who cannot be injured by investigation of his past history, so that the enemies of the party will be unable to rake up anything against him that nobody ever heard of*

Trumped in America:
Reflections on How Fascism Grows

before. If you know the worst about a candidate to begin with, every attempt to spring things on him will be checkmated. Now I am going to enter the field with an open record. I am going to own up in advance to wickedness I have done, all the women I have fornicated with, all the businesses I have stiffed, all the bankruptcies I have used to keep from paying just debts, and if any congressional committee is disposed to prowl around my biography in the hope of discovering any dark and deadly deed that I have secreted, why let it prowl.

In the first place, I admit that I treed an annoying grandfather of mine when I was 15. He was old and inexpert in climbing trees, but with the heartless brutality that is characteristic of me, I ran him out the front door of my father's mansion in Queens at the point of a shotgun and caused him to bowl up a front yard maple tree, where he remained all night, while I emptied buckshot into his legs. I did this because he snored. I will do it again if I ever have another

Trumped in America:
Reflections on How Fascism Grows

grandfather who snores while I am trying to sleep. I am as inhuman now as I ever was. I candidly acknowledge that I ran away from military service in Vietnam by getting five draft deferments and finally having a well-bribed doctor to certify I have bone spurs. After all, I am a scion of wealth and privilege, so why should I fight when there are plenty of flag-waving, Jesus-loving suckers willing to fight for my freedom to screw as many women as possible, not to mention all the business people I screw with my skilful con-man attributes. I wanted my country saved from those dirty old anti-capitalist communists, but let those unwashed flag-waving boys from poverty row save it for me. Then, when they come home they can shine my shoes.

My financial views are of the most decided character, but they are not likely, perhaps, to increase my popularity with the advocates of economic fairness. My single great fundamental principle of life is to get all the money I can in any

Trumped in America:
Reflections on How Fascism Grows

way I can. As for taxes, I don't pay any. That is for the poor suckers who don't make enough money to hire sleazy lawyers and crooked accountants.

The rumour that I buried a dead aunt under my winery grapevines was correct. The vines needed fertilizing, and my aunt had to be buried anyway, so I dedicated her to the higher purpose of saving me money. Does that make me unfit me for the Presidency? The Constitution of our country does not say so. No other citizen was ever considered unworthy of this office because he enriched his grapevines with his dead relatives. Why should I be selected as the first victim of an absurd prejudice?

I admit also that I am not a friend of the poor man. I regard the poor man, in his present condition, as so much wasted raw material. Cut up and properly canned, the poor might be made useful to feed some of my starving employees whom I pay as little as possible. I shall recommend legislation upon the subject in my first

Trumped in America:
Reflections on How Fascism Grows

Presidential message. My campaign cry will be, "Dissect the poor man and stuff him into Trump sausages which are great with Trump wine."

These are about the worst parts of my record, but they will let me stand before you as the man capable of making America great again. On that record I come before the country to ask for your vote. If my country does not want me, I will go back to Deutsche Bank rather than robbing the U.S. Treasury. But I recommend myself as a safe man, a man who starts from the basis of total depravity and proposes to be fiendish to the last dollar I can steal from you.

The above rendition is emblematic of what is happening today with the most uncouth, undisciplined, boorish, gross, crass, crude, ill-mannered, unapologetically inept buffoon to ever be called Mr. President. The modern political circumstance is one in which the political right refuses to compromise and the political left is always extending the hand of amelioration to only fall prey to the hard-nosed, self-righteous Republicans who have a my-way or the highway attitude that has stymied any real progress for nearly 50 years. Meantime, the cultural landscape has experienced a comedic infusion into public discourse on a scale quite possibly unmatched in U.S. history. We may in fact be living in a golden age of American political humour. Like it or not, the engagement of contemporary humorists in political and social dialogue has become central to the national conversation on essentially every policy matter of importance. Fortunately, most of the humorists are progressives who continually expose the hypocrisy and buffoonery of Trump. Unfortunately, it has had little effect on the unmitigated arrogance of Trump or his adoring fans who worship his every unpolished, unrefined, uniformed utterance.

The voices of contemporary humorists have become vital as the U.S. faces the real and rising spectre of fascism with the ascendency of Donald

Trumped in America:
Reflections on How Fascism Grows

Trump as a viable demagogue along with the extreme right wing political forces gaining influence and threatening a grasp on actual power that is unparalleled. Though unorganised, the community of humorists has created a vanguard against tyranny with popular voices enunciating an in-depth, while hilarious, analysis of facts. As with most artistic people, humorists have a social responsibility to elevate humanity.

The language of art and the legitimate press expands a vast microcosm of criticism compared to the barren senseless language of Trump's political regime. The simple-minded myopic Trump sees art and the investigative press as a threat. It therefore becomes incumbent to highlight a distinction or a direction in the language of art and the detail of a robust press, as the essential contributions of both are critical to calling out the dangers incumbent in an administration that will stoop as low as humanly possible to protect itself from thorough scrutiny by the thinking public.

Trumped in America:
Reflections on How Fascism Grows

It should be noted that the humorists may be encouraging laughter in the face of fascism, but they are not laughing it off, but rather using laughter to expose the tyrants who want to stifle dissent by proclaiming those immortal words – fake news. Who is the number one tyrant that monopolizes all the media? Trump is of course, but he, in fact, is nothing but a buffoonish narcissist who is being used by the privileged class to further their aims of enslaving working men and women to the oligarchy which has, with Trump's acquiescence, seized complete control of the U.S. government and is laying the groundwork with Trump's Supreme Court appointments to solidify that control for generations.

Humorists and satirists have always played a role in American public discourse. The expanse of humour in American life has historically shown the health of the democratic system in its ability to absorb criticism and analysis, even in its most pointed, satiric, sardonic or absurdist forms, or

Trumped in America:
Reflections on How Fascism Grows

when cast solely as entertainment. Active humorists are direct descendants of a significant ancestry whose work crossed into civic influence and engagement, and that is needed today.

It is not a stretch to claim humorists and journalists today have more platforms available than ever before to reach worldwide audiences. Contemporary humorists are significant enough in number and in reach that they have contributed, willingly or not, to filling a journalistic space left open in an era of transformative dumbing down of the media. This space is also being utilized by heinous groups for nefarious purposes as outright lies are passed off as news by right wing groups that never see two sides to an issue. Those who are easily manipulated never seek out variant sources for their information, but rather, they reinforce their prejudices by only seeking the news, entertainment and opinion which supports their point of view. When Ronald Reagan eliminated the Fairness Doctrine (broadcasters were required

Trumped in America:
Reflections on How Fascism Grows

to separate fact from opinion as a matter of law until repealed in 1987), he opened the airwaves created by new technologies to biased radical transitions in sustainable media business models, and the open appropriation of airwaves and content platforms to unabashed propagandists.

Today, any cogently thinking person should acknowledge the configuration of right wing thought with virulent religious evangelicalism has led to fascism getting a firm foothold in the United States. The rise of this ideology in America is not an academic exercise. It is a clear and present danger that may well not be reversed for many generations. The purpose of this book, as a matter of civic respect, is to lay bare the simple fact that fascism has arrived in America.

Chapter 4

Continually Cave In

The wealthy founders of the United States, first of all, were a pack of hypocrites who boldly proclaimed all men were created equal while denying the vote to women. O.K., so one could argue they were not hypocritical I suppose, because a woman's job was to serve men just like the millions of slaves in bondage at the time. In fact, 41 of the 57 signers of the Declaration of Independence were slaveholders, which made that equality statement even more hypocritical. Since they were all wealthy, the real reason they wanted to break away from England was to get out of paying taxes. (Sounds exactly like the rich today, who believe only the middle class should pay taxes.) However, to their credit, they did put certain caveats in the Constitution that were intended to make it impossible for a dictator to assume power. Having waged a prolonged and bloody revolution against a monarchy, they were well aware of the trappings of power and its foundations of absolutism. Still, it is ironic that a nation that sings the praises of the common man and discredits fancy titles like "his or her highness" insists on calling the President "Mr. President." How is that really any different than calling a royal leech, his or her highness? Frankly, if I were the President of the United States, I would have people call me Wayne. This aggrandizement by title-conferment is again the height of hypocrisy for a democratic nation.

Trumped in America:
Reflections on How Fascism Grows

The U.S. founders, however, at least directed wise and prudent oversight by establishing a robust system of checks and balances with free speech, separation of church and state (which has been blurred by both the Republicans and Democrats) and rule with the consent of the governed in order to keep power proportional through all levels and phases of government.

While cognizant of sealing off the path toward dictatorship, they were well aware that the system of democracy was not foolproof or without cracks, and today, with primarily one party rule, it appears that the founders did not foresee how easily one party, when it refuses any compromise whatsoever and when not in power creates extreme gridlock through ideological subterfuge, can allow a buffoon to assume almost dictatorial power. What the USA has suffered since the 1980's is gradual totalitarianism through rule by an oligarchy. A totalitarian grip on power has been manifested by a minority party (Republicans) which has used the

Trumped in America:
Reflections on How Fascism Grows

outmoded and undemocratic electoral college, along with incredibly effective gerrymandering (carving up Congressional districts to assure one party will dominate) to build a somewhat permanent ruling Congressional majority that cannot be dislodged through democratic means.

Fascism is not a term that the right wing will use as a self-identifier. However, sometimes they actually relish being called Nazis and fascists, even going so far as using the Sieg Heil salute. A careful examination indicates this fascism is rampant in the USA due to the oligarchy as a controller of government through the literal buying of politicians which was sanctioned by the Supreme Court in the Citizens United case, the utilization of religious zealotry as a manipulative technique, the highly propagandized instilling of patriotic fervour and the identification of certain groups as un-American. Trump even goes as far as calling Muslims, immigrants and African Americans vermin.

J. Wayne Frye

Trumped in America:
Reflections on How Fascism Grows

Fascism has a long history of being supported by the less educated and easily manipulated. Trump has brazenly proclaimed that he especially likes the uneducated. Why? Because he assumes that they are the easiest to manipulate. Unfortunately, he is somewhat on the mark, as diagnostic thought and cogent analysis are more likely to be manifested by those who are taught critical thinking skills. This is why Fox News and right-wing media are such a staple news source for the conservatives in America, because they do not use logic to support an issue. When emotion replaces critical thinking, the result can be anarchy, which is what often happens when conservative non-thinkers are baited by demagogues like Trump.

As a former university president and professor, I frequently incurred the wrath of my self-aggrandizing, arrogant, highly educated colleagues when they would assume a superiority mode by telling them, "Some of the smartest people I know dropped out of high school. How many of you can replace a carburetor, tune an engine or even change a tire? You do not judge intelligence by how many years of schooling a person has." That, in my opinion, is a profound observational analysis as, for example, I was often awed by a seventh grade educated father and grandfather who were the two smartest men I have ever known. They were so mechanically inclined that they could take apart a go-cart engine or a jet engine with comparable precession. They could read the National Enquirer or Shakespeare with equal understanding. They could even run a still and turn out alcoholic spirits that were the equal of any produced by a legitimate distillery anywhere in the world, and they had the business skills to run illegal alcohol from state to state without ever getting jailed for the illicit activity in which they engaged. What is my point? There are always exceptions to the rules in regards to critical thinkers. Unfortunately, the exceptions are far too rare in today's America.

Trumped in America:
Reflections on How Fascism Grows

Watching the low-waged, poor supporters of Trump enthusiastically rally behind someone who looks with disdain on them as the great unwashed masses unworthy to even tie his shoe laces makes one realize why the privileged class wants to destroy the depth of knowledge taught in public schools while using those schools to spew out propaganda to support patriotic indoctrination and servitude to an ideal that does not exist. Keeping people ignorant keeps them in chains to serve the privileged class. This is how the seeds of fascism are sown in a small percentage of the populace who will vigorously support an oligarchy that will crush them economically and politically right along with those that do not support them. No more than 35% to 42% of the American people support Trump, but those who do not support him are powerless due to the ability of the oligarchy to suppress all who dare question the economic and social order. The blind devotion of the uniformed to a demagogue is the lifeblood of fascism.

Trumped in America:
Reflections on How Fascism Grows

Fascism was invented in 1919 in Milan, Italy and it is actually fairly easily discerned if approached through critical analysis. Perhaps its most artful practitioner, prior to Trump, was one of its founders, Benito Mussolini. Since it has been around a long time, it is fairly easy then to see just how it is manifested.

Umberto Eco, noted Italian historian and novelist, published his essay on the 14 characteristics of Fascism in 1995. Below are his identifiers for fascism.

1. *The cult of tradition. "One has only to look at the syllabus of every fascist movement to find the major traditionalist thinkers. The Nazi gnosis was nourished by <u>traditionalist, syncretistic, occult (religious) elements</u>."*

2. *<u>The complete rejection of modernism</u>. "The Enlightenment, the Age of Reason, is seen as the beginning of modern depravity. In this sense, extreme fascism can be defined as irrationalism."*

Trumped in America:
Reflections on How Fascism Grows

3. *The cult of action for action's sake. "Action being beautiful in itself, it must be taken before, or without any previous reflection. <u>Thinking is a form of emasculation.</u>"*

4. *<u>Disagreement is treason</u>. "The critical spirit makes distinctions, and that is modernism. In modern culture the scientific community praises disagreement as a way to improve knowledge. Fascists reject this notion."*

5. *<u>Fear of difference</u>. "The first appeal of a fascist or premature fascist movement is an <u>appeal against the intruders</u>. Thus, fascism is racist by definition."*

6. *<u>Appeal to social frustration and a lack of respect for those in positions of power</u>. "One of the most typical features of historical fascism was the appeal to a frustrated middle class, a class suffering from an economic crisis or feelings of political humiliation and frightened by the pressure of lower social groups. (The poor as leeches.)"*

Trumped in America:
Reflections on How Fascism Grows

7. *The obsession with a plot by outsiders to weaken a nation*. *"The followers must feel besieged. The easiest way to solve the plot is the appeal to xenophobia."*

8. *The enemy is both strong and weak*. *"By a continuous shifting of rhetorical focus, the enemies are at the same time too strong and too weak."*

9. *Pacifism is trafficking with the enemy*. *"For fascism there is no struggle for life but, rather, life is lived for struggle."*

10. *Contempt for the weak*. *"Elitism is a typical aspect of any reactionary ideology."*

11. *Everybody is educated to become a hero*. *"In fascist ideology, heroism for the nation is the norm. This cult of heroism is strictly linked with the cult of death."*

12. *Machismo and weaponry*. *"Machismo implies both disdain for women along with intolerance and condemnation of nonstandard sexual habits from chastity to homosexuality."*

Trumped in America:
Reflections on How Fascism Grows

13. *Selective populism. "There is in our future a TV or Internet populism, in which the <u>emotional response of a selected group of citizens can be presented and accepted as the voice of the people.</u>"*

14. *Fascism speaks newspeak. "All the Nazi or fascist schoolbooks made use of an impoverished vocabulary, and an elementary syntax, in order to <u>limit the instruments for complex and critical reasoning.</u>"*

We now know what to look for, and it is easily spotted in the USA today by astute observers who see it being skilfully played out by the Trump administration. Trump's penchant for fascism is probably natural for someone who has such a fragile ego and feelings of inadequacy that he compensates for it with bluster and bullying. Having his name plastered on everything he can get his hands on is actually a way for showing his father, even though he is dead, that the son he kept bailing out financially has made it.

Trumped in America:
Reflections on How Fascism Grows

Any understanding of Trump's fascist tendencies can be traced to deep psychological problems which have plagued him probably since the first time his father told him how stupid he was. However, this book is not as much about Trump as it is about a nation that has turned to this despicable, self-doubting, egotistical, narcissistic buffoon to lead it into darkness disguised as light. To see how this happens one must have a thorough understanding of just how Fascism rears its ugly head.

The base definition of fascism as an ultra-nationalist, anti-democratic, right-wing form of governance employing intolerance, corporatism, irrational anti-intellectualism, false traditionalism, scapegoating, violence and militarism led by a demagogue figurehead has its roots in 1920's Europe. Fascism is, in reality, a means to totalitarianism. Central to its imposition is an easily manipulated, uneducated and fearful class of people who react with emotion rather than

J. Wayne Frye

critical thinking. The appeal to fear, anger, hatred, irrationality and anti-intellectualism is at the core of reaching people who see themselves as put upon by those who are different. Fascism's goal is to achieve power and enact totalitarian measures that will protect the privileged class while appealing to those who foolishly believe the bevy of lies perpetrated to keep them in bondage to the con-men and the few con-women who are in total control. Trump's lies are not lies, but rather alternative truths.

American hegemony has tried to turn the entire world into a capitalist monarchy of the oligarchy where the human equation is insignificant as all that matters is the bottom line, and for the USA, seeing its position of dominance diminished as other nations soften the harshness of capitalism has led to its gradual decline to Third World status for most of its citizens. Trump's tax cuts for the wealthy, derailing of business regulations and dismantling of environmental protections has thoroughly laid the groundwork for the oligarchic, white-collar fraudsters and banking classes to control every aspect of the American economy.

Donald Trump matches virtually every aspect of Mussolini's form, even down to his mannerisms of arrogance. Trump has managed to hold up a mirror to Mussolini's Italy, albeit in a uniquely American context. He has, through careful crafting, honed his skills as a con-man to actually convince his rabid followers that he represents the historical foundations of the USA in its adherence to religion as a guiding force. The pussy-grabber-in-chief is actually hailed by the evangelicals as a man of God who is anti-rationalist at his core, rejecting progress in education and intellectual inquiry, even proclaiming that evolution is only a theory. Trump, the manipulator supreme, is laying the groundwork for religious thought to pave the road to the totalitarianism that is his chief aim. In the USA, the cult of religion has been edging its way toward government dominance since it

Trumped in America:
Reflections on How Fascism Grows

moved its support to the Republican Party, which saw the fundamentalist religious zealots as a natural way to solidify a solid block of voters that would assist them in dismantling all the social legislation passed by Franklin Roosevelt and Lyndon Johnson. This unnatural alliance between the Jesus lovers and those who want to do just the opposite of what Jesus would do reaches a depth of moral depravity unparalleled in American history.

The attack on art and science is the glue with which American fascism cements itself to the body politic. The far right in the USA has long been opposed to both the arts and science. The most profound expression of this is the astonishing denial of climate change by Trump and his oligarchy allies. This, now, is the official position of the Republican Party, which steadfastly denies that climate change is a danger caused by mankind. Allied with religious zealots, apparently because they believe no matter what the catastrophe, their dear Jesus will somehow come to the rescue, especially of America, which is such a righteous nation.

Hostility toward the arts is just another profound example of how the right-wing fascists believe a highly educated thinking populace somehow is elite and incompatible with the aims of the oligarchy. They will never cut funds for bombs and bullets, but the arts are considered frivolous avenues of expression that serve no useful purpose.

The ignoring of public educational funding while promoting private schools has left crumbling intellectual infrastructure and a class of middle class educated people hopelessly in debt. Billionaire Betsy DeVos was not appointed Secretary of Education to improve public schools, but rather to dismantle them or make them into pre-incarceration holding pens for the poor who will be transitioned to the for-profit prison system. Look at schools and how children are constantly forced to queue up and follow strict rules and one can see that there is no room for creative thought.

Furthermore, teachers are not valued by American society. Rather, they are looked upon as glorified babysitters who make it possible for their parents to be free to toil in equally oppressive places. The recent anti-labour union decisions by the Supreme Court are partially aimed at making the workplace for teachers unpalatable, so they will no longer receive union protections. The elimination of tenure is next. Furthermore, it is only a matter of time until the teaching of creationism will be allowed, so that religion can be used to squelch independent thought.

Irrationalism is the core of anti-intellectual expression. The rise of conservative media and its insistence on the conspiratorial nature of those who oppose the right-wing is the perfect example of how the ignorance of the masses is played upon to construct "facts" that convince the people that somehow evil is lurking out there ready to swoop

Trumped in America:
Reflections on How Fascism Grows

down and devour all that glorious freedom which Americans erroneously think they have.

Facts are stubborn things, as the ability to separate nonsense from fact is increasingly difficult for a large percentage of Americans who never seek out opposing views; but rather, cling to sources that strictly reinforce their prejudices. For example, despite irrefutable proof that Iraq's weapons of mass destruction were complete fabrications by the Bush Administration, nearly 50% of Americans still believe Saddam Hussein had weapons of mass destruction, just as nearly 50% of the people think invading Afghanistan was justifiable because that is where the 9/11 hijackers were from, despite undeniable proof that 17 of the 19 hijackers were from Saudi Arabia. Facts simply no longer matter, and with Fox News and Sinclair Broadcasting parroting the oligarchy propaganda the mush-like minds of the evangelicals, flag wavers and true-believers in American superiority simply line up like sheep being led to the

J. Wayne Frye

slaughter. These enthusiastic flag-waving, amen-shouting easily manipulated patriots are doomed!

Perhaps the height of the fascism practiced by Trump is that great big beautiful wall he wants to build in order to keep out brown people. Trump's wall at the USA-Mexican border, along with mass deportations, the incarceration and separation of parents and children, the official barring of Muslims (except from Saudi Arabia which is the biggest supplier of oil) from entering the USA, fanatical racism, gender bias and misogyny, combined with abject bigotry toward LGBT people is the match that lights the fire of worship from Trump's adoring hordes. Trump's base, who fear that the white majority is at stake along with their ideas of what constitutes morality, as defined by that black book (Bible) of prejudice, all see him as the saviour of the white race. Trump makes racist rants that he barely masks, as he loves feeding his base the red meat of prejudice they all devour like it was a banquet set at the table of

Trumped in America:
Reflections on How Fascism Grows

tempestuous malarkey from the mouth of a God of discontent trying to arouse their ire.

Just because he is rich, does not make Trump a smart man. How many people, if they started out with two hundred million dollars, could be successful? However, he is an astute and accomplished con-man who knows how to appeal to a primarily white undereducated fascist-leaning political base of angry and violent discontents. Trump's base blames low wages, unemployment, economic inequality, diminishing opportunity and the economic stagnation on groups who are actually far worse off than they are in almost every economic measure. Yet, they fall for Trump's ruse that the brown people crossing the border illegally are the problem rather than the oligarchy which is in control of the economy and does not pay fair wages or their fair share of taxes.

While Bush's malfeasance may have led to the great collapse, Obama refused to hold the moneyed class responsible and put them behind

Trumped in America:
Reflections on How Fascism Grows

bars as he should have. So filled with hatred for the African American President, the delusional denizens of Trump supporters put all their faith in the Great White Hope to make America great again. How ironic that the struggling white middle class would actually place their hopes in one of the privileged class who is part of the criminal oligarchy which has seized all opportunity and completely crushed the working class.

Trump advocates keeping foreigners out as a way to convince his base that these foreigners are causing their economic pain rather then the oligarchy. Trump skilfully figured out that fascism appeals to the people who feel deprived of a clear social identity. Here, the fascist-leaning Trump supporters cling to country of birth as the only social bond within their perceived reach, as psychologically they desperately need someone to blame, and the oligarchy always effectively shifts fault, and the gullible willingly fall for this subterfuge. Trump lovers see the non-white hordes invading their scared land and are willing participants in the racist blame game.

Trump decries the rapist drug dealing Mexicans whom he says are flocking across the border to commit heinous crimes. Facts, of course, mean nothing to Trump or his supporters, as the facts actually show that native born Americans commit crimes at nearly three times the rate of legal and illegal immigrants. Conservative media has been central to supporting the myth of evil illegals cockily prancing about unleashing a reign of terror on law-abiding white folks. MS-13 (Mara Salvatrucha) is the gang most often used by Trump to stir up passion among his admirers. This gang did not originate in Mexico or Central America, but in Los Angeles in 1980, and was exported, with the support of the U.S. government to destabilize Central American countries that were embracing communism as a way to alleviate the suffering under dictatorships that were supported by America and the corporations that

Trumped in America:
Reflections on How Fascism Grows

were extracting vast wealth. Again, truth is sacrificed at the altar of Trump expediency. Obsessions with plots and conspiracies are the stock and trade for fascists who fill the gullible with wild tales that feed their appetites for blame.

In spite of the fact that illegals do not receive benefits, the Trump supporters continue to swallow the lie that these people live off welfare and receive social security benefits. In fact, these people pay into social security, but are, by law, barred from receiving social security in any form. However, Trump has successfully identified these people as the enemies of the working man, despite the fact that these people do jobs Americans will simply not do, because of the back breaking hard labour and the low pay.

By violence, military action, whatever the means, enemies must be identified and defeated by the lone man (Trump) capable of making things right. Of course, these identified enemies are not "real Christians" in the traditional sense that is only reserved for devoted, Jesus-loving white Americans.

According to Trump, only he has the ability, through his advocacy for white Christians, to bring the evil invaders to heel. These people are his scapegoats, and his supporters foolishly fall for the lies that pour out of his mouth like water over Niagara Falls. He, no doubt, laughs in private at just how easily he is able to fool so many people.

How strange that this narcissistic coward who received five deferments during the Vietnam War, and a bone-spur diagnosis the last time he avoided the draft, is made a hero by the flag-waving bastions of patriotic servitude. The buffoon does not even know the words to the National Anthem. Like Bush before him, he will gladly send others out to die for good old America, but if he has to defend the nation, no doubt, he would be found cowering in the corner of the Oval Office begging for mercy. He is the poster child of what is called the chicken hawk mentality that is so prevalent in

Trumped in America:
Reflections on How Fascism Grows

the Republican Party. Simply stated it is, "You must fight to the death to defend American values, but please don't ask me to do the same as my life is too valuable." Of those jingoistic Republican warmongers who brought you Iraq, for example, every single one avoided service in Vietnam, when they had the opportunity to battle America's perceived enemy. These are the chicken hawks who have bluster and patriotism only when they do not have to dodge the bullets.

American right-wingers press for violent military intervention in response to every conflict or political problem in the world. The fascist-loving manipulated patrons of men like Trump are impatient to die for the country and its exalted leader, and eventually Trump will ask for this loyalty from his brainwashed followers, who will dutifully line up to be cannon fodder. Remember, this is the man who boldly proclaimed in a speech that he could stand in the middle of Fifth Avenue and shoot someone and not lose any votes. His supporters roared with approval, taking that as a compliment to their undying, dedicated loyalty. Truthfully, it was an insult to what little intelligence they had, as he was saying they were so stupid they would follow him no matter how appallingly depraved he might be. One must ask how any reasonably intelligent person could bow before such vile turpitude. Yet, again and again his loyalists will accept any abominations of decency from this strutting peacock of arrogant self-serving ineptitude.

Trump is willingly supported by Republican enablers in Congress who have for years had a "my way or the highway attitude" that has effectively ground government to a halt unless the Republican Party is in control. One must actually admire their tenacity in standing up for their beliefs, no matter how deplorable they might be. This cannot be said of the Democrats who in a misguided effort at compromise continually cave in.

Trumped in America:
Reflections on How Fascism Grows

Chapter 5

Without Consequence or Accountability

The rise of fascism is predicated on four distinct elements. The first is simply that there is a vacuum within the political system caused by people's perception that things are working against them, and that what the system needs is a strong leader who will deviate from the norm and stir things up. Second is the adaptability of a demagogue to respond constantly to the prejudices of a minority of the populace by identifying a hated group to place the blame on. Third, fascism needs a strong figurehead capable of rousing the emotions of the disaffected, whose support will not waver no matter what despicable acts are performed by the leader.

Finally, for fascism to effectively grow, those who oppose it must be neutralized and rendered inconsequential through media and the body politic. Disaffection with the correct order, as defined by the fascists, can be defeated by branding the press as fake news and the opposition political party or parties as unpatriotic.

Donald Trump's position as the figurehead of American fascism in support of the manipulative oligarchy has been firmly solidified and the opposition is crying in the wilderness as his poll numbers remain stable, because those on the margins of support are gradually accepting the reality of where the nation is headed. There is a crowd mentality in play, and many people simply fear being on the outside looking in.

Trumped in America:
Reflections on How Fascism Grows

Trump is not a smart man in general, but in specifics, he is a phenomenal con-man who knows how to play to a crowd, especially a crowd of willing fascists. He loves big crowds, because he knows that the crowd mentality raises people's emotions. When one person starts to cheer, others are quick to join in. For example, why do television shows use a laugh track? Because they know that the show is not funny, but the laugh track is used to convince people to believe it is hilarious. They hear laughter so it must be funny, and they join in. Brainwashing is much simpler than most people imagine.

Donald Trump is now the laugh track of the Republican Party. He has managed to bring together a diverse group of uncharacteristic allies, the conservatives, libertarians, evangelicals, neo-cons, tea partiers, corporate élites, billionaires and a huge throng of disaffected uneducated members of the working class who actually believe they have a seat at the power table. The one thing they do have in common is that they are all primarily white and embrace a racist, xenophobic, paranoid view of the world.

There is no post racist society in America. For example, the Civil War never really ended for many southerners. They still believe their way of life was superior, and that the victorious north imposed an unjust peace on the poor old south where the "darkies" were really happy tilling the soil for their white masters. I am from North Carolina, which was part of the confederacy, and I see that attitude in much of my family to this very day. They still venerate those slave-holding, treasonous generals whose statutes grace public squares all over the south.

The complimentary component to the political vacuum in which most Americans live is the set of pre-conditions for which a fascist movement needs to fill the space. When Frenchman Alexis de Tocqueville toured the United States in the 1830's, the country was travelling the bumpy road of a new democracy. He traversed the USA and its western territories, observing the horrors of slavery in the south and genocide against Native Americans everywhere.

What struck de Tocqueville was the hypocrisy of that statement "all men are created equal." He saw grave danger down the road for a nation that practiced genocide and allowed millions to live in bondage. He summarized the concern for the USA in his book *Democracy in America*, as he observed that if you give every manipulated fool a say in the matter, the lot of them together may do the most foolish thing conceivable while following the most foolish demagogue imaginable. Way back then he visualized the possibilities of what the ignorant could raise in terms of misguided political structures in support of despots, as he saw a people who were like children in need of a firm parent to control them. These early Americans, he felt, actually craved a stern leader. The possibility was a terror beyond his imagination at the time of

Trumped in America:
Reflections on How Fascism Grows

his writing, as he sensed the growth of a nation capable of horrendous things from people who were so easily swayed by a manipulative leader.

Benito Mussolini, aided by Hitler, was credited with building fascism as a viable political force. However, both men used the American genocide against Native Americans as their model for how to identify a group of scapegoats for use as a tool to control the people.

Over the years, the American government's penchant for embracing fascism was evident in its use of the Monroe Doctrine to invade every Latin American country, even including a brief foray by General Pershing into Mexico in pursuit of the revolutionary Poncho Villa who had attacked the town of Columbia, New Mexico in 1916, burning it to the ground for what he saw as U.S. support for Mexican anti-revolutionary forces. This was only one incidence of problems created by American meddling in other nation's affairs to defend corporate interests that were raping Latin

Trumped in America:
Reflections on How Fascism Grows

American nations of natural resources. This meddling continues to this day, as corporate interests are always protected by the American government and defended by spilling the blood of the soldiers who foolishly sign up to fight what they think are the enemies of America, but what they are really doing is defending corporations that reap billions by stealing resources from nations all over the world.

Probably the most intelligent man to ever hold the Presidency, Franklin Delano Roosevelt, facing incredibly staunch xenophobic ultra-conservative opposition from the Republican Party in 1933 until his death in 1945, saw the beginning of a reactionary political party with sympathies for fascism. This penchant for embracing fascism was only mildly ameliorated during World War II when many American bankers like Prescott Bush (George W. Bush's grandfather) were fined, but never jailed, for violating the Trading with the Enemies Act.

Trumped in America:
Reflections on How Fascism Grows

The du Pont Chemical Company and General Motors, were major contributors to Nazi military efforts. In 1929, General Motors bought Adam Opel, Germany's largest car manufacturer. In 1974, a Senate Subcommittee on Antitrust and Monopoly heard evidence from researcher Bradford Snell proving that in 1935, GM opened an Opel factory to supply the Nazi's with "Blitz" military trucks. In appreciation for this help, Adolf Hitler awarded GM's chief executive for overseas operations, James Mooney, the Order of the German Eagle (first class). Besides military trucks, Germany's GM workers also produced armoured cars, tanks and bomber engines that would later be used against American soldiers. Of course, both corporations were playing two ends against the middle by also supplying military equipment to the U.S. Army. War is always good business for corporations, and American corporations could care less whose side they serve as long as there is money to be made.

J. Wayne Frye

Trumped in America:
Reflections on How Fascism Grows

Along with Du Pont and GM, the Rockefeller family's Standard Oil of New Jersey collaborated with I.G. Farben, the Nazi chemical cartel, to form Ethyl GmbH. This subsidiary, now called *Ethyl Inc.*, built German factories to give the Nazis leaded gas fuel (synthetic tetraethyl fuel) for their military vehicles. IG Farben had bought the patent for the cyanide-based pesticide, Zyklon B, which had been invented in Germany in the early 1920's and licensed to various companies, including the American Cyanamid Company for use in de-lousing incoming Mexican immigrants in the 1930's, and also to the infamous German company Deutsche Gesellschaft für Schädlingsbekämpfung, whose products were used in Holocaust gas chambers. Of course, after the war, du Pont pled ignorance to any knowledge of their products being used to exterminate Jews.

The du Pont family was actually so complicit that they formed a pseudo-fascist organization during World War II and James Farley, Franklin

Trumped in America:
Reflections on How Fascism Grows

Roosevelt's postmaster general, said the American Liberty League (organization founded by elite conservative American Republican businessmen and supported by du Pont to oppose FDR's New Deal) "ought to be called the American Cellophane League (du Pont invented cellophane wrap) because first it's a Du Pont product and second, you can see right through it." It was also known that du Pont had gained control of Remington Arms Company, which was involved in trade with Germany.

Embracing fascism is an American tradition going back in history long before the word was ever used. In the early 1950's, the poster boy for American fascism, Joseph McCarthy, destroyed people with hyperbolic name calling every bit as strident as Trump. Anyone that challenged him he called a communist sympathizer. His wild accusations eventually led to his demise, and he died from cirrhosis of the liver still shouting names of people he branded communists.

Trumped in America:
Reflections on How Fascism Grows

Other politicians over the years have used fear of communism as opposed to immigrants to arouse fascist sympathies among supporters. One of those was the only President to ever resign, Richard Nixon, who, before Trump, was the most corrupt of the many corrupt men who have held the office. Many of his cabinet officers and administrative assistants wound up in jail at a time when justice was a bit more prevalent. Of course, he was pardoned of all crimes, because despite what is said, Presidents are indeed above the law.

Although Nixon was a crook, when it comes to fascism, he was topped by another buffoon who got the Presidency in the 2000 election despite, like Trump, losing the popular vote. Fascism could probably not even be pronounced by George W. Bush, but by picking another five deferment draft evader as his Vice-President, Dick Cheney, he embraced the darkness represented by a man who had the bearing of Heinrich Himmler and the compassion of Josef Mengele. Cheney and Bush were a perfect combination, two cowards who evaded service in Vietnam, but were willing to dispatch other young men off to die after 9/11 in an ill-conceived revenge mission that has dragged on for over 17 years in a country from which not a single hijacker hailed, and then they had the audacity to send even more soldiers off to Iraq to die for a pack of lies about weapons of mass destruction concocted to excuse their need to pound their chests in victory over a Third World nation that had actually managed to keep terrorists in check. Just like Henry Kissinger, who should have been tried as a war criminal for Viet Nam, Bush and Cheney should have been hauled before the World Court in The Hague and prosecuted for crimes against humanity. However, the USA has never had to answer for any of its numerous war crimes, simply because it is the USA and is always excused for his heinous acts of barbarity all across the world. This is the way of a world that simply will never stand up to the USA.

Trumped in America:
Reflections on How Fascism Grows

A series of conditions for fascism has been fomenting for many years on the Republican political right wing in the USA, often aided by an inept Democratic Party. From the racist response to the civil rights pleas of African-Americans that saw wholesale attacks on marchers that were cheered on by the right-wing, the modern Republican party has parleyed this racism into a reliable block of votes that assures no matter what candidate they put up, Southerners and Midwesterners will blindly support the party of white fascists.

The development of a foreign policy centred around the frequent use of military power as a primary option for resolution of disputes, the massive movement to assure LGBT citizens are denied their rights, the branding of immigrants as vermin, the vilification of anyone who dare protest by kneeling during the National Anthem, the refusal to allow women to control their own bodies, the promotion of Christianity as

Trumped in America:
Reflections on How Fascism Grows

supporting the American ideal are all part and parcel of a uniquely American fascism.

In addition to the cultivation of the far right-wing over several decades, during the Bush administration several lines were crossed in shifting the country on to totalitarian ground which has made Trump possible, because Barrack Obama did absolutely nothing to dismantle the oppressive mechanisms of the state initiated by Bush and Cheney. Obama actually promoted the continuation of a massive system of pervasive and intrusive surveillance, affecting every law-abiding citizen that would make George Orwell stare in wide-eyed wonder at how his warning in the book *1984* is now part of every day America. The use of torture, extraordinary rendition, the denial of habeas corpus, the abomination of the Guantanamo Detention Centre and the ignoring of the Geneva Convention have all occurred under Republican and Democrat without consequence or accountability.

J. Wayne Frye

Chapter 6

The Prince of Darkness

The right wing oligarchy strengthened and grew as wealth became more concentrated at the very top of the economic ladder. Corporations now actually own the government. A few years ago, the bankers and unregulated gamblers in the oligarchy created systematic fraud on a scale in real dollars like none other in history, and caused a complete economic meltdown for which they will never be made to pay. The bill was picked up by the middle class, as Obama not only refused to hold Bush and Cheney responsible for crimes against humanity committed in two illegal wars, but also vehemently refused to prosecute the perpetrators of the worst financial calamity since the Great Depression. Meanwhile, he kept healthcare as a corporate run entity and the gulag in Guantanamo, proving that he was all talk and no action, as he continually caved-in to the right wing Republicans on almost every important issue. Even he, with his cavalier disregard for justice, made submission to authority central to what constituted a good American. America first, unilateralism, uncritical capitulation to mass surveillance and ardent militarism all fused into the civic and personal identity of every far right winger who stupidly believed Obama was a Muslim, as they could not see past the colour of his skin to realize that he was actually part of the oligarchy they worship. For that reason, they coalesced around Trump for complete capitulation to fascism.

Trumped in America:
Reflections on How Fascism Grows

The sharp increase in racial, social and economic scapegoating by the far right directed toward Muslims, Hispanics, African-Americans, women, the LGBT community and the poor, along with a systematic attack on voting rights and voting access, especially in areas with high concentrations of people of colour and the poor, assures that voting is restricted only to those who support the idea that traditionalism is under attack by a lunatic fringe left-wing that does not understand the real white America.

Just as fascism rose with its distinctive characteristics in Italy, Germany, Hungary and countless other places, it is now on a relentless march to overwhelm the USA and turn it into the fascist nation dreamed of by the oligarchy which has found its champion in Trump. The oligarchy has effectively taken control of all meaningful mechanisms of economic, political, media and military control in Trump's America. What opposition remains is ineffectual and unable to

Trumped in America:
Reflections on How Fascism Grows

coalesce around a unifying figure. The Democratic Party is so fractured that it stands little chance of fielding a candidate who can defeat Trump in 2020, and the investigation by the Special Prosecutor, Robert Mueller, is a complete waste of time, as even if collusion is proved, the Republicans will not vote for impeachment under any circumstances. Anyway, if Trump by some miracle was impeached, Vice-President Mike Pence is far worse than he is on a host of issues. Fascism in America is guaranteed for the future. Just as Franco in Spain and Salazar in Portugal demonstrated many years ago, consolidation of power is easy when you control the mechanisms of government with willing enablers, which Trump does. Thus, the USA is neither alone, nor terribly different than other countries in having embraced fascism, where the privileged class is given complete control by a group of people who are simply too weak-minded to see that they are being played for fools.

J. Wayne Frye

Trumped in America:
Reflections on How Fascism Grows

Over the course of the last forty years the oligarchy's pressure to tighten its grip on power has increased as it has manipulated the uneducated, angry, delusional and racists into unequivocally supporting it as long as it keeps them in fear that some evil outside force is destroying the American way of life that they have been propagandized into believing is somehow far superior to all other nations' way of life. The fusion of the oligarchy and the control of the few allied with the ignorant is the grease that oils the machinery of fascism now embraced by a significant minority in America. With so many seeds planted firmly in the ground of deceit, the harvest will be bountiful for the oligarchy.

Trump, who has never really worked a day in is life, is mentally farming the American right with precision as he harvests the evil which he has planted in the hearts and minds of those who do not have the intellectual capacity to see that they will be tossed into the shredder and ground up to

Trumped in America:
Reflections on How Fascism Grows

satisfy the needs of the oligarchy. The fundamental role of the fascist demagogue is to embody the notions of fascism and make them seem mainstream. The fascist is, at the core, a craving coward and an extreme bully who if confronted will hurl invectives at his detractors while rallying his brainwashed supporters to his side with cries of how unpatriotic and cruel those are who dare question his rule. History has shown that while they can bring chaos and immense destruction, ultimately the coward cannot stand against the courageous, but in America today, the courageous are in very short supply – witness that vast number of non-voters in 2016 who simply decided that since they were stuck with two despicable candidates they would not vote. I am one who decries always having a choice between the lesser of two evils, but that is why America got Trump. Sometimes, the lesser of two evils must be considered when the alternative is complete utter buffoonery and the embracing of fascism.

J. Wayne Frye

Trumped in America:
Reflections on How Fascism Grows

One could immediately discern Trump's fascist pedigree and cowardice as he encouraged using violence at his rallies, even going as far as saying he would pay the legal fees of anyone who attacked a demonstrator. The only way the fascist can win anything is to pick up a weapon or swing a fist, and in Trump's case his weapon is his bombastic foul mouth. This is one reason why most Trump supporters love their guns, because without a gun they are rendered impotent. Their number one achievement is having access to a gun which is an extension of their limp penis that gets erect only when they fondle a weapon. They are actually cowards, because rather than arm themselves with knowledge, they prefer a gun.

The current American Trump fascism reflects that practiced by the narcissistic, bombastic Mussolini rather than Hitler, as the later was actually intelligent. As the embodiment of American fascism, Donald Trump is communicating that fascism is acceptable to make

Trumped in America:
Reflections on How Fascism Grows

America great again. He has taken positions describing the willingness to effectuate mass deportations of non-white immigrants regardless of status, turning away people because of religious affiliation, punishing women for terminating pregnancies and under the guise of protecting Americans he is encouraging the erection of a southern border wall every bit as sinister as the Berlin Wall which was called an abomination by Americans for years.

Add to the above his intense hatred for any news organization but his vile propaganda spewing mouthpiece, Fox News, and you have a situation where at public events he points with disdain at journalists accusing them of being fake news for calling out his lies and deceit. The attack on the Capital Gazette that led to five journalists' deaths was barely mentioned by him, as he categorizes journalists who fact-check his lies as vermin also. He encourages and foments violence as a political tool by the forceful expelling of journalists from

Trumped in America:
Reflections on How Fascism Grows

public political events, openly stifles dissent by calling for the violent removal of detractors from public rallies, and has threatened control of the internet. Destructive turbulence is a regular occurrence at his rallies. He uses violence both as metaphor and as a call to action.

Trump has boldly admitted his proclivity toward committing war crimes, crimes against humanity, openly violating the Geneva Convention and ordering his military to do so as a matter of policy. He has advocated going after innocent family members of terrorists as punishment and has cavalierly asked why the USA has nuclear weapons if it is not willing to use them.

Through all this he has openly courted members of the Ku Klux Klan and the American Nazi Party, actually going so far as to say there are some good Nazis. White supremacist organizations are embraced by him, as he even refused to repudiate former Klan Grand Wizard, David Duke. Trump has regularly distributed lies and inaccuracies

Trumped in America:
Reflections on How Fascism Grows

from white supremacist social media and boasted that they are reliable news outlets while calling cable news networks like CNN and MSNBC fake news. He has routinely threatened riots, and his followers regularly make death threats to those who openly oppose him and/or his policies. He encourages intolerance, and his uniformed followers are so enamoured with him that they parrot his every word. This race-baiting and scapegoating to his mindless worshippers will eventually lead to an American Kristallnacht (Crystal Night). Kristallnacht was the time in 1938 when German authorities looked on without intervening, as mobs ransacked Jewish business and synagogues throughout Germany. The term refers to the mass of broken glass as the rioters broke windows in Jewish neighbourhoods.

In America today, it would be transgender organizations, gay clubs, mosques, Planned Parenthood, Hispanics and African-Americans who would suffer the brunt of bigoted anger as

Trumped in America:
Reflections on How Fascism Grows

Trump is constantly stoking the emotions of a delusional, willingly uninformed and purposefully paranoid segment of a populace that is incapable of rational thought. All his supporters can see are the brown and black hordes that they, after listening to Trump, believe are ruining their country.

Corporations, oligarchs, and members of the conservative political class are essential backbones of fascism, and although they are, at present, less than 50% of the population in the USA, they carry the clout of a huge majority when the nation's leader is willing to pander to their prejudices, supported by complacent members of the Republican Party. Meanwhile, the majority party (Democrats) does not have the courage or commitment to make a stand against the terror of the minority party (Republicans).

It is galling that the citizens who really have the best interests of the nation at heart will not stand up to those who want to tear down the fabric of

Trumped in America:
Reflections on How Fascism Grows

progressivism. The few demonstrations against Trump's fascist brutality are simply small blips on the radar screen of indignation. You do not change things by begging for mercy or obsequiously pleading with authorities to promote justice. Historians like to promote Martin Luther King as succeeding with non-violence, but that is not reality. Non-violence does not get anyone their rights! What happened was that radicals like the Black Panthers encouraged African-Americans to burn things down. Only when the ghettos were in flames and the privileged class feared their gated enclaves of privilege were next for ravaging did the nation throw a bone to the oppressed in the form of civil rights.

After fifty years, the pendulum is swinging back toward abject oppression of minorities, and fascists like Trump are blatant racists who must define enemies that are always non-white. It is necessary that they do battle incessantly, and always win, and even if they do not actually win

Trumped in America:
Reflections on How Fascism Grows

they lie about winning, because their fragile egos cannot accept defeat. They are lost if they stop causing turmoil, are overcome by indecision or if they begin discussions that might alter their direction. Trump's megalomania requires he continue his reality show non-stop, since it gets him the attention he craves. In fact, he would be lost without his megalomania that is fed by his desire to be aggrandized and worshipped. This trait is why he cannot accept the sparse crowd that attended his inauguration. Even though he knows the crowd was small, his fragile ego can not accept the fact that an African American actually drew a larger crowd than he did. His enablers compound his lies by parroting his fabrications as if enough people tell the lie, then it will no longer be a lie. How appalling that some lapdog like Kelly Ann Conway can actually come up with what she calls alternative facts to refute the truth for the man she grovellingly serves in complete supplication to his megalomania.

Trumped in America:
Reflections on How Fascism Grows

With Donald Trump, America has embraced its own Mussolini and like Italy, it is going to pay a high price for its flirtation with the Prince of Darkness.

Trumped in America:
Reflections on How Fascism Grows

Chapter 7

The Gullibility of Those They Oppress

Fascist movements have always been minority fringes that took hold through manipulation of ignorance and the cowardly actions of those who refused to stand up to tyranny. Just imagine what the history of the world could have been had Germans stood up to Hitler and refused to accept his xenophobic view of the world. And what if the majority of non-fascist Italians had the courage to stand up to Mussolini?

Trumped in America:
Reflections on How Fascism Grows

Fascism is on the rise in the USA, because there is no continuous concerted effort to arrest it. Fascism has taken over the Republican Party and fashioned it into a grievance-based dispenser of intolerance and hate. In a similar way, fascism in the 1920's spread because liberals and mainstream conservatives failed to take it seriously. Instead, they shrugged their shoulders and assumed it was simply going to fade from fashion eventually through the electoral process. Unfortunately, not fighting fascism has led to Trump being able to appoint two Supreme Court Justices which will for the next 20 to 25 years, at the minimum, bode ill for any progressive laws since the conservatives will have a majority that will continue to stick it to the poor and middle class, support corporatism at an accelerated pace, dismantle civil rights laws, destroy LGBT rights, bolster religious intrusion into government, eliminate a woman's right to control her own body and promote systematic discrimination based on race.

J. Wayne Frye

Trumped in America:
Reflections on How Fascism Grows

The right-wing and the Jesus zealots are bedfellows in the dreary darkness of patriotic fervour and religious virtuosity that has trapped Americans for many years in a status-quo of primal adherence to mediocrity. Meanwhile, with the exception of Muslim nations that share the same devotion to staying in the darkness rather than moving into the light, the rest of the world is progressing away from dogmatic adherence to religion that is exclusionary rather than inclusionary. Concurrently, the quasi-liberals in America are dumbfounded, confused and dismayed, unable to stand up to the tyranny that is represented by the right-wing fascists who have methodically hijacked the body politic and through subterfuge like gerrymandering and voter suppression made it impossible for liberals to mount any effective opposition.

The decadence of the wealthy, which is part of the capitalist system, signifies its presence day in and day out in the abject wickedness of the rich who keep getting more and more while the people they are trampling on keep enthusiastically cheering their oppressors, particularly the chief oppressor, Donald Trump. When Trump mocks a handicapped reporter, when he refers to Mexicans as vermin, when he brags about "grabbing 'um by the pussy," when he proclaims his sexual abuse accusers are too unattractive to warrant his attention, when he brags about paying as little tax as possible; his gullible, uncaring followers applaud and bow before his depravity as if it represented the second coming of Christ. There is a perverse sickness about worshipping such a despicable human being.

With so many ill-informed, uncompassionate, uncaring, xenophobic people fawning over Trump, one must logically ask if there is any way to combat this malicious evil. I will attempt to make some suggestions, but truthfully, I do not think there are enough Americans with the committed will to defeat Trumpism.

Trumped in America:
Reflections on How Fascism Grows

First, it is imperative to shed a clear light on how a progressive grass roots movement can be manifested. However, in a nation like America that is bound in the worship of an ideal that is a lie, that is committed to dogmatic, exclusionary religion and has a significant minority that simply stated are racists to the core, it makes one realize the monumental task it would be to alter a country that is trapped in a deep pit of darkness.

The biggest problem is the mindset of the average American who has been taught to think they are not poor, but temporarily disadvantaged soon-to-be millionaires. The masses actually believe this malarkey that America is a land of opportunity for the poor, where everyone has an equal chance at success. Ask the kids in south-central Los Angeles if they are equal to the kids in Beverly Hills. What fool actually believes the children from south-central are afforded the same opportunities as the children from Beverly Hills? The oligarchy protects its own.

Trumped in America:
Reflections on How Fascism Grows

The oligarchy supposedly despises socialism and promotes the capitalist ideal, but when the privileged class caused the economic crash, they were the ones embracing the socialist assistance from the government that bailed out their corporations. So, it is capitalism for the poor and socialism for the rich. It has been that way during most of the nation's history.

Keeping people ignorant of reality is what sustains the oligarchy's power. They oppose scientific inquiry and rational thinking, because that might help people see through the veil of deceit that protects those at the top of the economic ladder. They further their aims by promoting mass-minded supernaturalism (the Christian religion) and convince people that God is guiding the nation when a conservative is in power. When a non-conservative is at the helm, then Satan has infiltrated the government, and there will be hell to pay when the wrath of God is unleashed.

J. Wayne Frye

Trumped in America:
Reflections on How Fascism Grows

This is what makes it so difficult for progressives. Most have no religion, but in a play for votes they have to fake it, because the majority of Americans will simply not vote for an atheist. That makes it difficult for progressives to effectively stand up to fascism, because to defeat it there is an inherent need to get people to use their minds, which have been massaged with religion since childhood. Why do you think churches send out buses to pick up children for Sunday school? They know that if they do not get the young mind when it is easily manipulated, they have lost a convert. This is the same technique used by tobacco companies to lure youths into smoking, as they realize if they do not get a person by fifteen, the chances are the person will never be hooked to feed a drug habit by buying a legalized drug delivery system supplied by corporations. In fact, in order to release more highly addictive nicotine from the cigarette, manufacturers add ammonia. This is criminal, but since it is a corporation delivering the drug it is legal.

The truth has never been a particularly prominently displayed attribute with American politicians or the government, and with Trump, truth is now as rare as a dinosaur. Fighting against the bevy of lies from the mouth of the orange menace is no easy task when a fairly large percentage of Americans swallow his lies like Kool Aid handed out at the Jim Jones massacre in Guyana.

How then can the freedom-loving Americans left, who are too intelligent to fall for those lies, make an effective stand against this brazen attempt to use the uniformed to overthrow sanity? To tackle this difficult task, the majority of the progressives should first decide on the correct method of ascertaining truth. What should be their guiding philosophical outlook for correcting the drift toward totalitarianism that is supported by flag-waving, Jesus-loving, uniformed, racist, die-

Trumped in America:
Reflections on How Fascism Grows

hard fascists who have fondly embraced Trump as the saviour of the grand and glorious American civilization.

Truth is arrived at by critical scientific analysis, but this method is highly suspect by most Americans who have been brainwashed by constant patriotic propaganda to believe in the infallibility of their nation. There is a reason why history books hide the truth about American genocide, torture, support of authoritarianism, atrocities and horrible war crimes. Just like the Nazis did in Germany, history must be whitewashed to display Americans as somehow superior to all other nationalities. Himmler said, *"If you tell a big enough lie and keep repeating it, people will eventually come to believe it. The lie can be maintained only for such time as the state can shield the people from the political, economic and/or military consequences of the lie. It thus becomes vitally important for the state to use all of its powers to repress dissent, for the truth is the*

Trumped in America:
Reflections on How Fascism Grows

mortal enemy of the lie, and thus by extension, the truth is the greatest enemy of the state."

The lie of American superiority is promulgated through forced patriotism. There actually was a time when the National Anthem was not played at sporting events. But today, every sporting event is a patriotic display, which is promoted by the U.S. military as a way of instilling patriotism among the populace. Dare to kneel or sit in protest during the anthem and the long knives of the indignant propagandists will slice you apart. Go to a school in the morning and watch as children are coerced into standing dutifully with hand over heart to recite the lie about *liberty and justice* for all in the asinine Pledge of Allegiance. This is exactly what was done in Nazi Germany and Fascist Italy. Of course, as always, it is different when done by the USA. Go to a Trump rally, and listen in horror to the shouts of his loyal subjects, "USA, USA, USA." Then watch Trump as he blusters, chest out, waving his hands to conduct the symphony of

Trumped in America:
Reflections on How Fascism Grows

his subjects as in his ears the shouts of "USA, USA, USA," are no doubt translated into "Trump, Trump, Trump."

The whitewashing of history then is at the core of getting the populace to flounder in patriotic dribble emanating from the deceitful mouths of demagogues while they are being fleeced, lied to, manipulated and made into robotic like servants to the cause of the oligarchy.

Frankly, I believe that ignorance will always trump the truth in America, but I do wish those who still have the semblance of an inquiring mind will rise up in unison to shout out the cries of "USA, USA, USA" with a boisterous and unified cry of "Justice, Justice, Justice."

Historical analysis and knowledge stemming from scientific experiments and experience indicate that propaganda is a powerful tool in cooling the ardour of a populace for genuine change. It appears that people prefer to be led in ignorance that turns a blind eye to real hope and

Trumped in America:
Reflections on How Fascism Grows

change by clouding everything in emotional terms to appeal to those who are easily swayed to blame their problems on the immigrant or other groups who have infiltrated the sanctity of the nation and brought about ruin and decay. In America, the easily manipulated see the brown and black hordes as a threat to the character of the nation, just as Germans were taught to look upon Jews, Gypsies, communists and homosexuals as a threat to the glory of their country.

Evil, coercive antibodies have corrupted the body politic in America from its inception by a wealthy class that was kept somewhat at bay only between 1933 and 1980, but have emerged triumphant today in the complete subjugation of the masses who toil so the privileged can compile their riches on the backs of cheap labour. On one side is the bourgeois class represented by the Republican Party, the defenders of the political, economic and social order of the capitalist society, and on the other, the vast multitude of exploited

J. Wayne Frye

Trumped in America:
Reflections on How Fascism Grows

people under the leadership of a Democratic Party that only pays lip service to economic and social justice. The interests of the privileged class and the working class stand antagonistic to each other, but the working class has few champions that stand up for it, while the privileged class has both parties in its pocket. To this end, they have captured the will of most to fight against the inevitable triumph of those at the top of the economic order. In fact, there is little, if any hope that the middle class and poor will ever rise up in unison against those who have enslaved them.

If true change is to occur, the idea that there can be compromise between the two classes must be trampled under the indignant righteousness of the revolutionary boots of the working class. It is impossible to fulfill the hopes of the working men and women as long as a privileged class exists. Only by systematically eliminating privilege for the oligarchy can there be hope for the working men and women of America. Privilege must be tossed over the cliff of discontent, and with it the nepotism that assures those at the top of the economic ladder cannot pass their privilege on to their progeny.

The thinking, ideas and values of one class are in perpetual struggle with those of the other class. It is unfortunate that the economically poor church-going adherents for Jesus do not realize that they have more in common with the LGBT community than the rich oligarchy that is using religion and its accompanying bigotry as a tool of enslavement. Religion is not about God, it is about control that convinces the poor that one day the last on earth will be first in heaven and that they will walk those streets of gold in that special place in the sky. Meanwhile, the rich are laughing at the gullibility of those they oppress.

Chapter 8

Reaping Rewards from Insanity

The state power being in its hands, the oligarchy has an edge over the proletarian class, but the proletarian class is nobler by virtue of being oppressed, even if not always being more progressive. What the brainwashed denizens of left and right both need is a more revolutionary approach to eliminating the privileged class. It is the oligarchy which actually promotes peaceful revolution, because it knows that any real progress cannot be achieved through peaceful means. Justice never has and never will be instituted through purely peaceful actions. As borne out by history, unfortunately, death is almost always required for any real progress toward equality. As alluded to earlier, it is not the peaceful revolutionary who facilitates change, but the fiery advocate who knows power comes from the barrel of a gun or a Molotov cocktail. The oligarchy will never peacefully transfer its power.

People actually are deluded if they believe fascism can only exist within a government. It has infiltrated the economic field much to the detriment of workers. Witness the recent Supreme Court decision in *Janus vs. AFSCME*, which will literally destroy public unions and will likely have a detrimental effect on the private sector unions. The Supreme Court's conservative majority enthusiastically endorses fascism in the workplace in support of the oligarchy, even increasingly extending its influence over social movements.

Trumped in America:
Reflections on How Fascism Grows

The easily manipulated right-wingers in America lack the historical and scientific understanding of the real character of fascism, which they are enthusiastically embracing in the person of Donald J. Trump. They are unable to conceive that fascism can be established fully even under the cloak of democracy as they march like the jack-booted SS in support of a man whom they think is going to return America to a glory that never really existed. These people are totally ignorant of the sordid history of fascism in both pre-war Germany and Italy, and in fact, would, in most cases, have been vigorous supporters of Hitler and Mussolini.

Although fascist states were defeated in World War II, fascism was not. It is alive and well in today's America supported by that 35% to 42% of the population that is desperate for someone to lift them out of the economic rut they have been trapped in since Ronald Reagan solidified the idea that greed is an enviable trait.

J. Wayne Frye   131

Trumped in America:
Reflections on How Fascism Grows

Capitalism and fascism work in perfect tandem, as they are never mutually exclusive. A look at National Socialism (a name selected by Hitler because it was more benign than National Oligarchic Capitalism) in pre-war Germany shows that propagandists are able, through a charismatic leader, (yes, Trump is charismatic to his unthinking base) to get the people to go along with authoritarianism.

Fascist culture is highly conducive to the capitalist economic structure developed in Germany, because any opposition was either physically suppressed or diminished through psychological intimidation. It took Hitler and Mussolini both about four years to achieve their aims of a rabid core of citizens for support, while neutralizing any opposition through intimidation and strong-arm tactics. This same method is being fined-tuned today by Trump and his puppet masters who are turning lose the political base on all opposition.

J. Wayne Frye

Trumped in America:
Reflections on How Fascism Grows

Since the merging of religion and politics in open defiance of the Constitution, the oligarchy has used religion skilfully to convince the white Christians that the very core of America is under attack by Muslims and atheists who will trample Jesus beneath their feet. This cultivation of a group that believes God is somehow guiding America as his promised land actually looks upon Trump as a man of God. The "pussy grabber and chief" is venerated and praised by evangelicals who discount his every abomination of all Jesus stood for. This is modern religion in America, so obsessed with getting prayer back in school, eliminating abortion and protecting gun rights that they are willing to overlook any transgression by their dear leader.

These attempts at combining religion with politics are helping with the dissemination of spiritual beliefs and various supernatural ideas that are heatedly opposed to rationalism, which explains part of the Trump phenomena.

Trumped in America:
Reflections on How Fascism Grows

It has become the main characteristic feature of the emerging fascist culture in the USA to cloak evil under the guise of religion. Throw in a few *"amen's,"* and the Trump base gobbles up the lies like a man finding an oasis after being in the desert for forty days and forty nights.

Blind obedience, a sense of mechanical discipline, clandestine and covert prejudices are the foundations of fascism which must be constantly and skilfully promulgated to keep supporters in constant emotional frenzy. The desire for free discussions, debates and exchange of views must be eliminated, because critical thinkers are to be feared.

The leaders and the rank and file of the right-wing are constantly displaying a notable lack of philosophical tolerance. The attitude for a patient appraisal of opposite views and criticisms is disappearing as Trump vows to pay the legal fees for those who perpetrate violence against any who dare question his veracity.

J. Wayne Frye

Trumped in America:
Reflections on How Fascism Grows

Blind Republican fanaticism and dogmatism are increasing as it appears party members do not feel any prick of conscience in making continuous slanders and fabricating fanciful stories in order to vilify those who stand against the march toward totalitarianism. All these actions are reminders of how Goebbels, Hitler and Mussolini fomented the emotions of their followers to squelch all opposition. Furthermore, Republicans have undermined union values, which helped to free the working class from the dark confines of the old wage slave mentality environment in the era of mass unionization. These rights have been eroded since the previous "star President," Ronald Reagan, fired 12,000 air traffic controllers and barred them from ever being employed by the government again, because they had the nerve to strike for improved pay and benefits. The anti-feudal workers' liberation struggle basically came to a halt under Reagan, who ironically rose to power as head of the Screen Actor's Guild Union.

Trumped in America:
Reflections on How Fascism Grows

With Reagan as President, the exploitation of the working class was fully realized and rubber stamped with approval by a government which decided corporations were more important than people. This approach assured that the USA would no longer promote social progress and revolutionize the mental framework of the society to lift up the working class. Reagan's trickle down theory that stated a hand-out to the rich would trickle down to the middle class and poor has been around nearly forty years now, and the middle class and poor are still waiting for the trickle to reach them. Tax cuts for the rich are the panacea that Republicans have espoused continuously to the detriment of economic fairness. These unethical and debased moral values have not ever spread downward to the majority of Americans, but the Republicans, wrapping themselves in the flag and Jesus have managed to actually convince the marginalized that they will eventually reap rewards from this insanity.

J. Wayne Frye

Trumped in America:
Reflections on How Fascism Grows

Chapter 9

Who Their Real Enemies Are

The essence of all religion is blind faith in personified or abstract supernatural forces exercising control over worldly things and events. Since scientific reasoning strikes at the root of this blind faith, the working class in the USA have turned their backs on a progressive role and have made themselves into protagonists of spiritualism to, they think, serve God, but in truth they are serving the oligarchy.

Trumped in America:
Reflections on How Fascism Grows

The exploiters of the ruling class always conspire to dupe people with the opium of religion in order to prevent them from correctly diagnosing the cause of their present exploitation and become conscious of the laws of development and social progress. The fascists preach spiritualism to keep the blind faith in religion alive. The Trump adorers have wilfully turned the religion of peace into a cult of violence to gag the voice of opposition and to preserve the oligarchy which has skilfully manipulated them to solidify their position of privilege. To quote that imminent scholar, Wayne Frye, "There is no fool like the fool who cheerfully lines up for his own ball and chains."

If various social movements in the USA really want to build up equality, they must realize the historical truth that it is impossible to establish equality in its true sense without overthrowing the present capitalist and fascist system through revolution under the proletarian leadership. Those

Trumped in America:
Reflections on How Fascism Grows

believers in progressive cultural movements who comprehend that socialism is the only way for social progress and for people's liberation must realize that change is not achieved by meekly begging for justice. It must be demanded, and if not given, then the alternative is revolution.

The reactionary role of Trumpism is to put an end to mutual civil discussions and debates and seek to stifle opposition viewpoints by physical force under whatever slogans and banners they may muster, and to brand anyone who stands against them as unpatriotic and treasonous.

The circumstances of society, the economy and geopolitics are firmly in the hands of the oligarchy, but foolishly, the opposition Democratic Party refuses to fight dirty as their opposition continuously does. Conservative politicians must actually be admired for never wavering in their determination to support tax cuts for the wealthy while cutting benefits for the middle class and poor. They do gave guts!

Trumped in America:
Reflections on How Fascism Grows

The circumstances today are similar to what happened in pre-war Germany in many, but not all ways. The most identifiable similarity is the scapegoating of minorities, religious outliers and immigrants in order to shift the blame from the real culprits, the oligarchy. In Germany, the shock troops fought cultural battles in response to a strong leader who appealed to their prejudices. In the USA, the vile individual and group threats against non-whites are manifested every day as Trump supporters, like the Nazis, think they have been given a green light to attack those who do not represent what they believe are "real Americans."

Trump is a master at theatrical machismo, with his bluster and braggadocio combined with the deliberately provocative, demagogic language that sweeps aside rational, evidence-based arguments and any perception but his own. He is a man bereft of any semblance of shame and will stoop as low as possible to motivate his base to impetuously feed his ego.

J. Wayne Frye

Trumped in America:
Reflections on How Fascism Grows

While Trump's fascism promotes America first as a rallying cry for those who have been left behind for so many years, the rhetoric also turns American against American. You either side with Trump and his supporters or you pay a price. Although a New Yorker born and bred, and educated at an Ivy League School, his strident rhetoric is anti-cosmopolitan and anti-intellectual. He denounces global social democracies while supporting American capitalism, which is the most vile form of capitalism, blaming ordinary people's woes on alien evil doers and past ineffective Presidents in gross language that is implicitly anti-immigrant, anti-Hispanic and anti-African-American, as a view of the world is presented that is centred on fears of national disaster and the decline of the nation. These fears can only be halted by one man who can reverse the horrors in which whites are demographically overwhelmed by inferior people, races and immigrants. That man, of course, is Donald Trump.

Trumped in America:
Reflections on How Fascism Grows

This is old-time fascism masked with modern methods orchestrated by one shallow, self-serving, egotistical megalomaniac, and the nation is dangerously underestimating his potential for catastrophic harm as he is aided by equally self-serving enablers. The world underestimated the evil of fascism with Hitler and Mussolini, and it seems to be doing the same with Trump, who just as Mussolini was used by Hitler, is being used by Vladimir Putin.

The mainstream conservatives, facing little electoral challenge from a left that has been rendered impotent, feels like they can control Trump. They accept the drift of their own voters to a blustering, bullying anti-immigrant, anti-democratic demagogue on the right, as they have been rendered utterly powerless because of Trump's effective playing of his base which has surrendered their souls in service to his narcissism. They are spineless and lack the courage to stand up to a man who has successfully manipulated

J. Wayne Frye

Trumped in America:
Reflections on How Fascism Grows

35% to 42% of unthinking Americans to rally behind him in lockstep with his aim not to make America great again, but to use his office for personal enrichment and ego-gratification. His supporters are so enthralled by his child-like rhetoric of exclusion that they are willing to forgive him any abomination. Those who humbly bow before this cretin of craftiness are similar to those who line the streets to cheer for the leech-like royalty as they parade by the unwashed masses in their gold carriages and their finery. One wonders how people can be so stupid to cheer those who enslave them. However, the Presidents of the United States have always been feted as royalty, and the very term Mr. President speaks to the need of people to worship at the altars of those in high position. That is not democracy. That is willingly accepting yourself as somehow being inferior.

These Trump worshipers accordingly espouse the right's priorities and accommodate its hate speech because the majority of them are, unfortunately, racists who feel threatened by the browning of America.

The result, for America, is a poisoned public life and a so-called democracy reduced to the tyranny of Trump and his minions that find emotional satisfaction and power in a violent, resentful rhetoric that satisfies those who are too wrapped up in hatred to realize that they, along with those they hate, are paying a similar price as freedom ebbs ever so slowly away into the darkness where the oligarchy sits counting their money and smiling with glee at how easy it is to distract the people from who their real enemies are.

Trumped in America:
Reflections on How Fascism Grows

Epilogue

A Just Man

The whole aim of practical politics is to keep the populace alarmed (and hence clamorous to be led to safety) by menacing it with an endless series of hobgoblins, all of them imaginary.

..................................*H.L. Mencken,1918*

Mencken's observation is as germane today as it was in 1918, only the media used to convey the message has changed, and demagogues are more effective now than back then. Truth is always the

Trumped in America:
Reflections on How Fascism Grows

first casualty when fascism takes hold, and in the United States the strategy is the same as that followed in pre-war Germany and Italy. American laws and courts are supposed to provide machinery which can be used to prevent any infringement upon the democratically constituted rights of the people, but the law has been subverted by Trump, and his two conservative appointments to the Supreme Court, along with the other three solidly conservative justices, will assure that he will not face any consequences for the crimes he has committed. The man may be a moron, but he is a wily moron who will simply not be dethroned from his perch where he displays an arrogant disregard for justice.

The Italian and German people made the fatal mistake of tolerating the activities of Mussolini's and Hitler's storm troopers that enforced conformity until the two despots grew so strong that they seized all power and crushed every sign of democracy. Ironically, the very people who are

Trumped in America:
Reflections on How Fascism Grows

shouting "USA, USA, USA," believing they are defending the nobleness of their country might as well be shouting, "enslave me, enslave me, enslave me."

As I watched the Evangelical Christians line up in unison behind Trump as he campaigned around America, the hypocrisy of these Jesus lovers was mindboggling. Here is a man who is the polar opposite of everything Jesus stood for, but as Trump mocked handicapped people, boasted of grabbing women by their genitals, encouraged crowds to commit violence, called law-abiding citizens rapists and murderers because of their skin colour, bragged about his immense wealth while not paying taxes as his followers do, these Christians shouted with glee in support of this abomination to all that is just. As a result, I was moved to write a poem that describes how people are unable to see that the support they give to a charlatan will eventually come back, as the saying goes, "to bite them in the ass."

Trumped in America:
Reflections on How Fascism Grows

The Cloak Man
By J. Wayne Frye

Into the town walked a man in a long dark cloak.
He smelled of sulphur, this swaggering bloke.
He saw a tall dark-skinned man in the square,
Who had a beard and scraggily chestnut hair.

The man in the dark cloak stared into his eyes,
And therein he saw where true kindness lies.
Oh, but the man in the cloak harboured more,
For he had some evil for this town in store.

The man with the chestnut hair moved on.
In a sudden flash he was abruptly gone.
The man in the cloak was not there for good,
As he pulled over his head the cloak's dark hood.

With little hands the man pointed at the jail,
And pronounced to all their country had failed.
He turned to a Mexican and an Asian as he said,

Trumped in America:
Reflections on How Fascism Grows

"These ones on your generosity have fed."

"I'll lock them up in that jail a long while.
Support me and you'll love my style."
The townspeople cheered the hooded man on.
And afterward, the Mexican and Asian were gone.

The whites there had long been discontented,
And held anger that was suddenly vented.
People of colour they thought were to blame.
So they supported Cloak Man to their shame.

Cloak Man on another of colour laid his hand,
A poor old soul who came from another land.
And Cloak Man felt no sympathy or love or grief,
As he paraded him away to the whites' relief.

The next day's sun looked mildly down
On roof and street in the quiet little town.
And stark blackness was in the morning air,
As Cloak Man pranced about on the square.

Trumped in America:
Reflections on How Fascism Grows

And whites cried, "Are you done now?"
He replied, "No, others are far more foul."
Then they smiled and stood amazed,
For now their prejudice was raised.

Then one citizen cried, "This evil is a shame."
But he was the only one who forward came.
Cloak Man said to all standing there,
"It's either for me or him you can declare."

Most declared for Cloak Man with glee,
While those opposed began to flee.
He appealed for the blood of those not white.
Cloak Man blotted out compassion's light.

Cloak Man said, "And what of the Jew?
With him what say you that we must do?"
The crowd said loud and clear, "Kill! Kill!"
"Yes," said Cloak Man, "it'll be a thrill."

People of colour were dispatched with ease,

J. Wayne Frye

Trumped in America:
Reflections on How Fascism Grows

As Cloak Man stood there so pleased.
He smiled and shouted to them one and all,
"Now we must build a grand, great wall."

Cloak Man in all his selfish egomania that day
Had absolutely everything his own way.
Only white people were left in town
As they felt a saviour was for all found.

The crowd gathering bricks for the mighty wall,
Stopped and stared at a man comely and tall.
He walked in peace and love among the flock,
But so blinded they embraced his love not.

The Cloak Man stood before a cross,
As he said, "Stand with me or you are lost."
With black hammer and long nails in hand,
He said, "We will crucify this man?"

Forgotten was former reverence showed him,
As Cloak Man had made things look grim.

J. Wayne Frye

Trumped in America:
Reflections on How Fascism Grows

Nailed to the cross at Cloaked Man's request,
Around the crucified man townspeople pressed.

Compassion sacrificed at the altar of bigotry,
The white people embraced their own misery.
The man on the cross sighing simply confessed,
"I die not for you, but for your selfishness."

"Who was this man in our beloved land?"
The crowd asked of Cloak Man.
With a sinister snarl, Cloak Man replied with glee,
"Idiots, you crucified Jesus again can't you see?"

There is no reason why knowledgeable, thoughtful people, attacked by a pernicious ideology, cannot counteract such propaganda with greater and more intelligent propaganda to educate the people to the advantages of democracy and to what fascism really means. However, in today's toxic political environment those on the right simply refuse to seek out alternatives to the daily

Trumped in America:
Reflections on How Fascism Grows

propaganda that is effectively spewed out by Fox News and other right-wing sources that are the purveyors of a sinister ideologically driven agenda that far too many people embrace simply because they had rather let others do their thinking for them. Most people do not realize that freedom simply does not exist in a vacuum. It must be tenaciously fought for and staunchly defended with more than the deadly weapons of war. It must be fought for with the power of the mind, a mind that can distinguish between lies and truth, a mind that can distinguish between manipulative rhetoric and compassionate concern, a mind that can distinguish between a vile demagogue and a genuine leader.

In the end, an aroused populace must stand against the tyranny in mass and be willing to suffer dire consequences in defence of liberty. It seems to this author that what Henry David Thoreau talked about years ago in his *Civil Disobedience* essay is apropos today: *"Under a government which imprisons unjustly, the true place for a just man is also a prison."*

Trumped in America:
Reflections on How Fascism Grows

Bibliography

Davies P. and Lynch, D. (2002). The Routledge Companion to Fascism and the Far Right. Routledge. pp. 1–5

Blamires, C. World Fascism: a Historical Encyclopedia, Volume 1(Santa Barbara, California: ABC-CLIO, Inc., 2006) p. 140–41, 670.

DuPont (E. I. DuPont de Nemours & Co.) http://www.corporatewatch.org.uk.

DuPont (E. I. DuPont de Nemours & Co.) http://www.corporatewatch.org.uk.

El-Shabazz, M. "Malcolm X" http://www.geocities.com/SoHo/St...

Engelbrecht H. Merchants of Death, 1934

"Explosives," Dupont website: http://heritage.dupont.com/float

Gerard Colby, Du Pont Dynasty, 1984

Gertman, L. Fascism in America, 2016.

Griffin, R. . Fascism. Oxford, England: Oxford University Press, 1995. pp. 8, 307.

Hartley, John (2004). Communication, Cultural

Trumped in America:
Reflections on How Fascism Grows

and Media Studies: The key concepts (3rd ed.).Routledge. p. 187. ISBN 9780521559829.

Hawksworth, K. (1992). Encyclopaedia of Government and Politics: Volume 1.

Higham, C. Trading with the Enemy, 1983.

Johnston, Peter (12 April 2013). "The Rule of Law: Symbols of Power". The Keating Center. Oklahoma Wesleyan University.

Kallis, A. The fascism reader. New York, New York: Routledge, 2003. p. 71

Larsen, Stein Ugelvik, Bernt Hagtvet and Jan Petter Myklebust, Who were the Fascists: Social Roots of European Fascism (Columbia University Press, 1984; ISBN 978-8200053316), p. 424, "organized form of integrative radical nationalist authoritarianism."

Mann, M. Fascists. Cambridge University Press, 2004. p. 65.

Turner, Henry Ashby, Reappraisals of Fascism. New Viewpoints, 1975. p. 162. States fascism's "goals of radical and authoritarian nationalism".

Wilhelm, Reich (1970). The Mass Psychology of Fascism. Harper Collins. ISBN 978-0285647015.